Dialectics, Power, and Knowledge Construction in Qualitative Research

This book is about going beyond a. ....y. ɪne research literature in social sciences is full of apparent dichotomies, such as the dichotomy between qualitative and quantitative approaches; "reality" and "multiple-realities"; ontology and epistemology; researchers and participants; the right and wrong conduct of research; and sometimes even between the goals of research and the ethics of research.

Throughout the book, it is shown that adopting a dialectical approach, which attempts to integrate apparent contradictions and opposites at a higher level of abstraction, may serve as a way out of the twin horns of such dilemmas. To begin this journey, the authors start with the classical dilemma of the relationship between "reality" and "knowledge," as a common divide between the quantitative and qualitative epistemological paradigms, and the philosophical assumptions underlying them. To illustrate the understanding of the relationship between knowledge and reality, metaphors of "maps and territories" are used as a framework for the dialectical construction of knowledge.

This book will be valuable to a diverse readership, including scholars interested in epistemology and philosophy of science and research methods, mainly from qualitative traditions. It will also be of interest to quantitative researchers as well, including supervisors of graduate students, lecturers and, most importantly, students and researchers-to-be.

Adital Ben-Ari is a professor of social work at the School of Social Work, University of Haifa, Israel.

Guy Enosh is an associate professor of social work at the School of Social Work, University of Haifa, Israel.

Routledge Advances in Research Methods

For more information about this series, please visit: www.routledge.
com/Routledge-Advances-in-Research-Methods/book-series/RARM

Dialectics, Power, and Knowledge Construction in Qualitative Research

Beyond Dichotomy

Adital Ben-Ari and Guy Enosh

Routledge
Taylor & Francis Group

LONDON AND NEW YORK

First published 2020
by Routledge
2 Park Square, Milton Park, Abingdon, Oxon OX14 4RN

and by Routledge
605 Third Avenue, New York, NY 10017

First issued in paperback 2020

*Routledge is an imprint of the Taylor & Francis Group, an
informa business*

© 2020 Adital Ben-Ari and Guy Enosh

The right of Adital Ben-Ari and Guy Enosh to be identified
as authors of this work has been asserted by them in
accordance with sections 77 and 78 of the Copyright,
Designs and Patents Act 1988.

British Library Cataloguing-in-Publication Data
A catalogue record for this book is available from the
British Library

Library of Congress Cataloging-in-Publication Data
Names: Ben-Ari, Adital, author. | Enosh, Guy, author.
Title: Dialectics, power, and knowledge construction in
    qualitative research : beyond dichotomy / Adital Ben-Ari
    and Guy Enosh.
Description: Abingdon, Oxon ; New York, NY : Routledge,
    2020. | Includes bibliographical references and index.
Identifiers: LCCN 2019016036 | ISBN 9780415833400
    (hardback)
Subjects: LCSH: Qualitative research—Philosophy. | Social
    sciences—Methodology.
Classification: LCC H61.15 .B45 2020 | DDC 001.4/2—dc23
LC record available at https://lccn.loc.gov/2019016036

ISBN 13: 978-0-367-72691-1 (pbk)
ISBN 13: 978-0-415-83340-0 (hbk)

Typeset in Times New Roman
by Apex CoVantage, LLC

Contents

PART THREE
Relational Implications – Power Relationships,
Power Differentials, and Reciprocity   55

Introduction

This book is about going beyond dichotomy. The research literature in social sciences is full of apparent dichotomies, such as the
dichotomy between qualitative and quantitative approaches; "reality" and "multiple-realities"; ontology and epistemology; researchers
and participants; the right and wrong conduct of research; and sometimes even between the goals of research and the ethics of research.
Throughout the book, we have endeavored to show that adopting a
dialectical approach, which attempts to integrate apparent contradictions and opposites at a higher level of abstraction, may serve as a
way out of the twin horns of such dilemmas. To begin this journey, we
will start with the classical dilemma of the relationship between "reality" and "knowledge" as a common divide between the quantitative
and qualitative epistemological paradigms (Lincoln & Guba, 2013)
and the philosophical assumptions underlying them. To illustrate our
understanding of the relationship between knowledge and reality, we
use the metaphor of "maps and territories" (Korzybski, 1933) as a
framework for the dialectical construction of knowledge.

Part One: Maps, Territories, and the Ontological/ Epistemological Stance

In Part One we will discuss the theoretical and practical implications
of dialectics on knowledge construction.

In **Chapter 1 – The Map is Not the Territory: From Ontology
to Epistemology in Knowledge Construction** – we assert that every
research act is an act of creating a new way of understanding and
perceiving, a new map of the territory; as Alfred Korzybski stated,
"the map is not the territory." This simple phrase reflects our basic
constructivist stance. The map represents reality, but it is not reality
itself. All of our knowledge may be thought of as maps – symbolic

representations of our perceptions of reality. In a nutshell, this dictum captures the essence of the distinction between ontology and epistemology and the relations between the two.

In **Chapter 2 – Dialectics: A Mechanism of Knowledge Construction** – we rethink "structure" as we move from a dyadic system of a research relationship to a triadic system. Traditionally, research relationships were known to have included the exchanges between researchers and participants. We claim that such relationships are only partial representations of the research's interactions. That is, we have considered several systems of relationships including those between researcher and participants, between research and the phenomena under study, and between participants and research phenomena. Such a triadic system is a valuable source of knowledge and should be considered as such.

Part Two: Personal Implications of Reflectivity, Researchers' Reflectivity, and Participants' Reflectivity

In **Part Two**, we will discuss the personal implications of reflectivity for the different parties in the research. Thus, we will focus on reflectivity from both the researchers' and participants' perspectives as well as from the interaction between them, as they pertain to the research process. We will also discuss the relationship that may develop between researchers, research participants and other stakeholders in the research process.

In **Chapter 3: Reflectivity Reconsidered,** we refer to reflectivity as representing both a contemplative stance and an intentional activity. The contemplative stance indicates a basic curiosity, a need to know, to understand. The intentional activity indicates an active search for differentness – the quest for what Bateson (1972) has termed "a difference that makes a difference." In this chapter, based on our understanding of the dialectical construction of knowledge we posit different ways in which an active search for a sense of differentness may occur. Those ways of searching for differentness are all directed at creating dialectical tensions geared towards noticing differences that make a difference. For example, they include taking different perspectives on the same phenomenon, using the "figure-ground" dialectic of Gestalt psychology, searching for apparent contradictions, searching for "knowledge holes" and "missing information," to name a few.

In **Chapter 4: Reflectivity and the Researchers' Perspective,** we claim that *researchers' reflectivity* involves reflecting upon the ways in which our own values, experiences, interests, beliefs, and political commitments shape our identities. It also involves the need to be aware of one's social context and the influence of societal and ideological constraints on previously taken-for-granted practices. This self-reflexive position is only one key to the understanding of how we construct the maps of our comprehension of the phenomena we are studying. In addition, we also suggest different levels of analysis at which researcher's reflectivity may occur, from observation, through informants' accounts, through text deliberation, to contextualization and reconstruction.

In **Chapter 5: Reflectivity and the Participants' Perspective,** we claim that common perspectives of the reflective process tend to represent such processes as procedures of discovering or rediscovering some "pre-existing" reality. Such processes are procedures of defining, delineating, and constructing insights and understandings by participants and researchers. While most literature on the subject has mainly focused on the reflective processes of researchers, we emphasize that reflection and reflexivity also occur when participants are asked to narrate their stories, reminisce about experiences, or express opinions. Any similar interpersonal communication that occurs in qualitative (as well as quantitative) interviews are based on the participant taking a reflexive stance, pondering his or her perceptions (maps) of what is or was, and deciding how to relate those to the interviewer. In other words, interviewees construct their maps of reality through intra-personal as well as inter-personal interactions, communicative acts, and self-reflection. They may decide on the emotional and reflective distance they take from their memories of experiences; they may decide on the formula that they use to relate their experiences, behaviors, emotions, and thoughts, through various linguistic modalities, such as different levels of abstraction, using stories, using metaphors, etc.

In **Chapter 6: Ethical Differences and Similarities as Sources of Reflection and Knowledge Construction**, we demonstrate how applying a "sense of differentness" to the identification of ethical differences and similarities between researchers and participants may serve as the starting point for the production of knowledge through exploration and reflection, conflict, negotiation, and argumentation. For heuristic purposes, we have organized the analysis around four conceptual alternatives regarding agreement or disagreement with respect to the moral stances of researchers and participants and discuss them with regard to ontological, epistemological, and moral levels of analysis.

Part Three: Relational Implications – Power Relationships, Power Differentials, and Reciprocity

In **Part Three** we will adopt a reflective perspective, examining the interactions between researcher and participant vis-à-vis the phenomena at hand, and use it as an additional source for knowledge construction. Over the years, it has become commonly accepted that knowledge is constructed by both researcher and participant in an interactional and reflective process, the outcome of which is the creation of shared meanings. Interactions between individuals consist of sets of exchanges in which they attempt to make sense of and interpret their own and their partners' verbal and nonverbal behavior within a certain framework of understanding. Research has both content and contextual dimensions. Although researchers may be intellectually conscious of the significance of context as a source from which meanings and knowledge can be derived, many are inclined to focus mainly on content. By disregarding the contextual dimension, the relational aspects between researcher and participants (i.e., modes of communication, power differentials, moral stances, etc.) and their role in the research process would have remained neglected.

Every study may be perceived as an arena reflecting the undercurrents of interaction, worldviews, moral stances and power differentials between the researcher and participants. Those undercurrents may impede the knowledge construction process by undermining the research partners' motivation for an in-depth exploration of the issues at hand. Yet, they may also be a motivating factor in exploring differences and thus become a source of knowledge production. We argue that paying attention to, analyzing, and using differences between the researcher and participants may prove to be the cornerstone for/ to understanding the substance and process of knowledge construction. Thus, we should perceive research not necessarily as shared and agreed-upon meaning-making endeavors, but rather as ambiguously complex processes with multiple levels of "differences interrupting differences" (Scheurich, 1995, p. 243).

In **Chapter 7: Research Relations and Power Differentials: From Resistance to Collaboration and In-Between**, we discuss research relationships from the perspective of status and power. Power has been defined as the ability to manipulate others' thoughts or actions (Kelly, Burton, & Regan, 1994; Millen, 1997). Underlying this discourse is the notion that researcher–participant relationships are primarily dichotomous, asymmetrical, and provide the researcher with an unequal position of power vis-à-vis the participant (Kvale, 2003; Limerick, Burgess-Limerick, & Grace, 1996). This is mainly due to the different social status most researchers have as compared to their research participants, and the patronizing attitude researchers have applied to the participants. This patronizing approach has often led to active or passive resistance on the part of the participants, not only towards the researcher, but to the research process as a whole. Within this context, we maintain that the relationships between the researcher and participants may be conceptualized in terms of a continuum ranging from full cooperation to antagonism and conflict, and delineating five interaction styles: (1) full cooperation; (2) negotiation over reality construction; (3) deflection and power games; (4) discrepancy between declared agreement and actual participation in research; and (5) overt refusal or conflict. We will use each and every interaction style as a source of knowledge construction.

In **Chapter 8: Frames of Reference and the Control of Knowledge**, we discuss the interrelations of knowledge and power. Control over knowledge shifts the foci of power between researchers and participants in unexpected ways that twist and turn the plot, possibly leading to a different view of power differentials, consisting of the control of knowledge, and relating those to the previously presented nature and attributes of the research relationships. Given that the major goal of the research endeavor is the production of knowledge, power relations in qualitative research might be conceived as the power to have an impact on the sources, processes, and outcomes of knowledge construction.

In **Chapter 9 – Reciprocity: The Nature and Attributes of Research Relations and Power** – we trace the move from dialectics of power to reciprocity in research relations. Whereas in the past research participants were mainly considered to be providers of information (informants, subjects) and as means to the end of knowledge acquisition initiated by the researcher, shaping fundamentally asymmetrical relations, more recent conceptions of the research relationships attempt to portray a more symmetrical research relationship between researchers and participants. As a reaction to the initial asymmetric and potentially exploitative nature of research relationships, over the years, a new trend has been developing in which a quest for symmetry of relationships has become a driving force and sometimes a goal of research (Kvale, 2003; Limerick et al., 1996).

We claim that equality between research parties is unrealistic because each plays an entirely different role and is motivated by different goals. Adopting conceptions of the research relationship as symmetric or asymmetric tends to create interminable futile attempts to achieve symmetry where it does not, and cannot, exist. Rather than viewing an egalitarian research system of relationships as reflecting a first-order change, we suggest introducing a second-order change into the system of research relationship. Viewing the interaction as reciprocal in nature promotes a schematic change, allowing a second-order change to take place. Rather than restricting ourselves to either symmetrical or asymmetrical relationships, understanding that these relations are reciprocal fosters a synthesis between the two previously opposing views. Using a dialectical reasoning mode, we switch from an either/or perspective to a both/and perspective (Basseches, 2005).

In the **Epilogue: From Dialectics to Dialog Across Liminal Spaces**, we expand our perspective to other ethical and political implications of our conceptualizations, by examining relationships with other stakeholders in the research process, such as funders, research gatekeepers, monitoring systems (e.g., ethical review boards), etc. All of these require the researcher to reflect upon one's relationship with each and every one of them and the conflicting demands that arise from these relationships. From this perspective, this entire book is about research ethics, just as much as it is about reflexivity and dialectics. Thus, the final chapter of the book will review how the basic approach we have delineated in earlier chapters, regarding dialectical reflexivity as a tool of examination and reciprocity as a goal of relationships, applies to the researcher's relationships with other research partners and stakeholders.

References

Basseches, M. (2005). The development of dialectical thinking as an approach to integration. *Integral Review*, *1*, 47–63.
Bateson, G. (1972, 2000). *Steps to an ecology of mind: Collected essays in anthropology, psychiatry, evolution, and epistemology*. Chicago, IL: University of Chicago Press.
Kelly, L., Burton, S., & Regan, L. (1994). Researching women's lives or studying women's oppression? Reflections on what constitutes feminist research. In M. Maynard & J. Purvis (Eds.), *Researching women's lives from a feminist perspective*. London: Taylor & Francis.

Korzybski, A. (1933). *Science and sanity: An introduction to non-Aristotelian systems and general semantics.* Englewood, NJ: Institute of General Semantics.

Kvale, S. (2003, August). *Dialogical interview research – Emancipatory or oppressive?* Keynote speech given at the 22nd meeting of the International Human Science Research Conference. Stockholm, Sweden.

Limerick, B., Burgess-Limerick, T., & Grace, M. (1996). The politics of interviewing: Power relations and accepting the gift. *Qualitative Studies in Education, 9,* 449–460. doi:10.1080/0951839960090406.

Lincoln, Y.S., & Guba, E.G. (2013). *The constructivist credo.* Walnut Creek, CA: Left Coast Press.

Millen, D. (1997). Some methodological and epistemological issues raised by doing feminist research on non-feminist women. *Sociological Research Online, 2,* 3. Retrieved from www.socresonline.org.uk/2/3/3.html.

Scheurich, J. (1995). A postmodernist critique of research interviewing. *International Journal of Qualitative Studies in Education, 8,* 239–252.

Part One

Maps, Territories, and the Ontological/ Epistemological Stance

1   The Map is Not the Territory: From Ontology to Epistemology in Knowledge Construction

Reality, and the ways we construct our understanding of it, is a core issue of the research endeavor. The concept of research implies an attempt to understand "something." This "something" can be referred to as "reality." Despite this fact, questions such as what is "reality" – is it independent of the research act, can it be known, or researched at all – arise. Such questions are commonly referred to as *ontological* questions. These are a related set of questions that deal with the nature of "knowledge." Does it represent reality? Is it subjective? What are the relationships between knowledge and reality? Such questions are commonly referred to as *epistemological* questions. Ontological and epistemological questions have occupied philosophers' and researchers' thoughts for thousands of years (Hughes, 1997; Rorty, 1979), and it would be beyond the scope of this book to go into all the different ways in which they have been asked and answered. Instead, at this point, we will focus on our own ways of understanding the dilemma and our solution for it. On the one hand, an "objectivist" approach to knowledge would claim that reality exists independent of the researcher and the research act, and the knowledge developed by the researcher is but a representation of such reality. On the other hand, a "subjectivist" approach would claim that all knowledge is dependent on the knower's perspective. It would claim that each researcher brings to the research act his or her way of perceiving reality, the explicit and implicit assumptions of their culture, the impact of their interaction with research participants, etc. Hence, all "knowledge" is subjective, contextual, and there is no way to ascertain the "truth" value of such knowledge (Hughes, 1997; Rorty, 1979). Obviously, one could find support for each of those opposing claims, as well as harsh criticism of each.

We find that the way to navigate between the horns of the subjective and objective dilemma lies with the constructivist approach. From this perspective, every research act is an act of creating a new way of understanding and perceiving, a new map of the territory, while keeping in mind Alfred Korzybski's assertion that "the map is not the territory"[1] (1933, pp. 747–761). Indeed, this simple phrase reflects our basic constructivist stance. While the map represents reality, it is not reality itself. All of our knowledge may be thought of as maps – symbolic representations of our perception of reality. In a nutshell, this dictum captures the essence of the distinction between ontology and epistemology and the relations between the two. Our basic conviction is that "reality" exists as a multifaceted entity, which may be perceived through various representations, none of which mirrors reality but, instead, presents a model of relating to, or working with, the specific aspect of reality. We never know "reality" to be in and of itself. We know our representations of it. While ontology refers to "reality," our ways of representing reality are summarized in maps – epistemology. It is clear that the relationship between reality and the maps, ontology and epistemology, is not arbitrary. However, the decision about *what* map to construct or choose is pragmatic in nature and emanates from the function intended. Thus, we need to decide what aspect of the "Territory" we are interested in and, according to this distinction, we will construct the right (or wrong) map, thereby providing us with the crucial information needed. To make this metaphor more concrete, if we were to take a trek in the Himalayan mountains, we would want a very detailed trail map. Such map would give us some knowledge about what to expect in terms of distances, road types, heights, and other relevant information. However, if we would like to map out agricultural plantings, the types of maps we would like to have are weather and precipitation maps and a geological map informing us of the types of soil, among others. All maps of the same territory, while being very different, represent our understanding of different aspects of the same reality. Thus, it is important to keep in mind that different maps, or different points of reference, may refer to the same reality, even though they are from different perspectives that emphasize different characteristics. Similar maps may differ in the level of detail and level of accuracy in their depiction of the relevant attributes of the territory.

From the perspective of the interaction between ontology and epistemology, we maintain that while it is not completely arbitrary, the decision about which map to choose, and how to draw it, depends on the human being, and his or her goal – in other words, the intended function. Furthermore, as has been stated and demonstrated by constructivist scholars, our modeling of the world, while it may be idiosyncratic and subjective, is geared towards functionality, enabling our understanding, and is constrained by context, language and social environment (Liu & Mathews, 2005).

The development of constructivism has been carried out in two seemingly separate lines – the first one emphasizing the individual level of developmental cognitive constructivism and intrapersonal constructions of knowledge ("Radical constructivism" as presented by writers such as Piaget, Bruner, von Glaserfeld, Watzlawick, and others), while the other emphasized the role of social context and environment in constraining and contributing to the construction of knowledge ("social constructionism" as presented by writers such as Vygotsky, Kuhn, and Gergen). The differences in emphasis have led some critics to suggest that those approaches are divergent and form two competing metatheories of knowledge construction – one focused on individual processes and the other on collective or social processes (e.g., Gergen, 1991; Talja, Tuominen, & Savolainen, 2005). However, a close reading of the writings of the major proponents of each "school" or "metatheory," indicates that the sources of divergence are based only on different, rather than essential, emphases.

From a radical constructivist standpoint, Ernst von Glaserfeld (1989) suggests that the need to construct new knowledge arises when we encounter a "perturbation," where our model of the world does not operate the way we expect it to.[2] He further differentiates between two levels of learning or knowledge construction. First the "utilitarian" action plan, and second, the reflective abstraction that entails an understanding of the rules by which the action plan operates. He points out further that although most of our learning occurs in a context of communication, still, "language users must individually construct the meaning of words, phrases, sentences, and test" (p. 132). Therefore, while we construct our knowledge within the context of culture, language, norms of thinking and scientific paradigms (Berger & Luckmann, 1966), it is still at the individual level that the construction is developed, and the more abstract the understanding, the higher the odds are for discrepancies and "perturbations" between communicators, to exist. Understanding the subjective nature of knowledge construction can help bridge such discrepancies (von Glaserfeld, 1989). In other words, recognizing that our language, understanding, and knowledge are simply maps that may differ from one another and may be more or less accurate, even though they refer to the same "external reality" but to completely different aspects of it, is crucial. As Liu and Matthews (2005) state, "implied in these comments is a dualist polarizing of the individual and the social, as only when the individual and the social group are viewed as fundamentally separate from each other, can one be emphasized, whilst the other is overlooked" (p. 391). Indeed, we suggest that in order to overcome this dualistic dichotomy, one should adopt a dialectical approach, which would transcend the splitting of individual and society, and of mind and reality, through an understanding of the interplay between those seeming polarities, and realizing that they represent different maps to the same territory.

Thus, our goal in this book is to construct useful maps that may guide the readers in their understanding of the research process and research relations, as being based on different and sometimes seemingly contradictory perspectives. We refer to the process of integrating seemingly different or contradictory perspectives a dialectical mode of knowledge construction. In order to do so, we have structured the book around the two major interrelated themes: processes of reflectivity and research relations. Whereas processes of reflectivity may be thought of as depicting the personal or individual aspects of the construction of knowledge through the research process, be that the participants' reflectivity or the researchers' reflectivity, research relations depict the social environment and context of the research process and the ways in which these relations are constructed and shape reflectivity and the knowledge is constructed. As we demonstrate throughout the book, we cannot understand the process of knowledge construction without relating to both the individual level of reflectivity as well as the complex levels of interaction between researchers and participants.

Notes

1. The origin of the metaphor supposedly goes back to the statement by Eric Temple Bell that "the map is not the thing mapped" (Bell, 1933).
2. We will elaborate on this issue and its applications for qualitative research later on, when we discuss our concept of "sense of differentness" (Chapter 2 and Chapter 3).

References

Bell, E. T. (1933). *The magic of numbers*. London: United Book Guild.
Berger, P.L., & Luckmann, T. (1966, 1991). *The social construction of reality: A treatise in the sociology of knowledge* (No. 10). London: Penguin.
Gergen, K. (1991). *The saturated self*. New York. NY: Basic Books.
Hughes, J. (1997). *The philosophy of social research* (3rd ed.). London: Longman.

Korzybski, A. (1933). *Science and sanity: An introduction to non-Aristotelian systems and general semantics*. Englewood, NJ: Institute of General Semantics.

Liu, C.H., & Matthews, R. (2005). Vygotsky's philosophy: Constructivism and its criticisms examined. *International Education Journal*, *6*(3), 386–399.

Rorty, R. (1979). *Philosophy and the mirror of nature*. Princeton, NJ: Princeton University Press.

Talja, S., Tuominen, K., & Savolainen, R. (2005). 'Isms' in information science: Constructivism, collectivism and constructionism. *Journal of Documentation*, *61*, 79–101.

von Glaserfeld, E. (1989). Cognition, construction of knowledge, and teaching. *Synthese*, *80*, 121–140.

2 Dialectics
A Mechanism of Knowledge Construction

The research endeavor is rife with contrasts, apparent contradictions, and clashes of interests and perspectives. From a positivistic/objectivist epistemological perspective, such clashes give rise to the need to "choose sides" and decide which one is true. From a subjectivist or "inter-subjectivist" perspective, different truths can co-exist or there is no concept of truth. In this book, we contend that an alternative approach to the dilemma of realism vs. subjectivism with all their variations would be a dialectic approach. A dialectic approach claims that apparent opposites on one level can be united or synthesized at a higher level of conceptualization. Therefore, the present chapter examines dialectics, delineating its epistemological aspects and emphasizing its significance in the construction of new knowledge. Let us start with the following questions: What is dialectics?; Does it exist in and of itself in the "real" world?; or, is it a useful construction of human thought, helping us understand the world we live in? These questions are the prevailing questions, not only in the present chapter but for the entire book, as well.

From the perspective of constructivist epistemology, dialectics may serve as the grand paradigm that serves as a useful way of creating knowledge, as it trains us to depart from the given, self-evident and trivial to adopt a multi-level, integrated, beyond-dichotomy, perspective. Using von Glaserfeld's (1989, 2013) metaphor, dialectics may be thought of as a master key that can open many locks of knowledge, and enables us to usefully construct our understanding of the research reality.

The Traditional Perception of Dialectics as Ontologically Based

Traditional approaches to dialectics were ontological in that they referred to dialectics as representing an intrinsic "objective" reality that exists in and of itself (see, for example, the work of Roy Bhaskar on Critical Realism) Archer, Bhaskar, Collier, Lawson, & Norrie, (2013). Dialectical conceptions of reality and ways of knowing can be found in both Western and Eastern traditions. From this perspective, reality is defined as dialectical in as much as it comprises ongoing processes of change, assuming that oppositional forces form the basis of all phenomena, and that change is constant and ongoing. These assumptions converge into the understanding that contradictions drive change. They create an ongoing tension between challengers, forces, or themes that negate or oppose one another, yet are simultaneously interdependent.

Scholars who adopt a dialectical perspective in order to understand interpersonal relationships (Baxter & Montgomery, 1996; Ben Ari, 2012; Montgomery & Baxter, 1998; Rawlins, 1989, 1992) generally accept that opposites normally co-exist within the same phenomenon, as well as in conflicts and contradictions. They maintain that change is an internal process that often leads to the unity of opposites and that it takes place through conflict and opposition. Assuming a dialectical perspective results in the constant search for contradictions within people or situations, as the main guide to what is going on and what is likely to happen. In particular, we may treat dialectics as a basic attribute of human conduct that manifests itself, individually (Ben-Ari & Dayan, 2008), or within the context of familial and interpersonal (Ben-Ari, 1995; Montgomery & Baxter, 1998), or intimate relationships (Ben-Ari, 2012; Ben-Ari, & Adler, 2010).

Epistemological Considerations: Dialectics as a Mode of Reasoning

We could say that men thought in a dialectical way before they were even aware of doing so and before its etymology, definitions, and applications were studied. Dialectical thinking is a mental process comprising or synthesizing facts, views, and goals of opposing stances (Basseches, 2005; Friberg & Öhlen, 2010). It refers to the ability to view issues from multiple perspectives and to arrive at the most reasonable reconciliation of seemingly contradictory information and postures. It is a form of analytical procedures that pursue knowledge as long as there are questions and conflicts. An apparent contradiction (conflict) along with dialectical reasoning can initiate the process through which knowledge is produced. Overall, we can delineate the following fundamental assumptions behind dialectical reasoning: First, contradiction is a temporary state that will be replaced by integrated or synthesized thought. Second, the progress of thinking is linear and logical, and moves from being a contradiction to synthesis.

Third, integration or synthesis is at a higher level of cognitive functioning (Baltes & Staudinger, 1993; Benack, Basseches, & Swan, 1989). However, such a depiction of the assumptions behind dialectics is missing an important ingredient – change. Dialectical thinking is based on, and emphasizes, change; instead of talking about static structures; it talks about process and movement. It is about looking for alternatives and widening our horizons, reiterating the notion that we should not be deceived by what we perceive to be "known or fixed." Instead, it prompts us to look at how it changes. In this context, scholars have emphasized dialectics not as a problem-solving method, but rather as playing a significant heuristic role, by providing a set of warning signs against dogmatism and the narrowness of thought. Applying the dialectical approach to qualitative inquiry suggests that discrepancies and opposites found at one level of analysis may be reconciled at a higher level of conceptual integration. During this process, the researcher becomes attuned to "news that makes a difference" (Bateson, 1979, 2000).

Emphasizing change in this context and the appreciation of change by the researcher warrants some further elaboration on the meanings of change. In their classical book *Change: Principles of problem formation and resolution*, Watzlawick, Weakland, and Fisch (1974) distinguished between first-order and second-order change, implying that change can be understood to occur at two levels. First-order change is *constrained by* the rules of the system, while second-order change is *geared towards* the rules of the system. Working within the frameworks of systemic and communication theory, they claimed that first-order change relates to positively changing the individuals in a setting in an attempt to fix a problem. Second-order change refers to systems and structures involved with the problem. Basseches (2005), who contributed significantly to the development of modern age dialectics, defines dialectics as a second-order change, as a "movement through forms," which is in contrast to "movement within forms" (first-order change). Following Baseeches, we contend that "movement through forms" refers to the dialectical ability to view issues from multiple perspectives, and arrive at the most reasonable reconciliation of seemingly contradictory information. It is a form of analytical reasoning that produces knowledge as long as there are questions, conflicts, and apparent contradictions. In this context, first-order change is the tacit understanding of change consistent with an existing system, while second-order change is the conscious modification of an existing system (Bartunek & Moch, 1987). The relevance of this assertion is that first-order change helps maintain existing knowledge and understanding, while second-order change is geared towards replacing them and, as such, is responsible for the production of new knowledge. In dialectical terms, a second-order change synthesizes two opposing stances into a higher level of conceptual analysis. The synthesis itself becomes a new thesis, which in turn is negated by a new antithesis, thereby producing a new synthesis in an endless process of knowledge production (Ben Ari & Enosh, 2010; Enosh & Ben-Ari, 2010).

To summarize, in this chapter we highlighted dialectics and its contribution to processes of knowledge construction in qualitative research. We have emphasized its relevance to understanding reality, as well as its fundamental role in producing knowledge and deepening our understanding of the world we live in.

References

Archer, M., Bhaskar, R., Collier, A., Lawson, T., & Norrie, A. (2013). Critical realism: Essential readings. Routledge.

Baltes, P.B., & Staudinger, U.M. (1993). The search for a psychology of wisdom. *Current Directions in Psychological Science, 2*, 75–80.

Bartunek, J.M., & Moch, M.K. (1987). First order, second order and third order change and organization development intervention: A cognitive approach. *Journal of Applied Behavioral Science, 23*, 483–500. doi:10.1177/002188638702300404.

Basseches, M. (1980). Dialectical schemata: A framework for the empirical study of the development of dialectical thinking. *Human Development, 23*, 400–421.

Baseeches, M. (1984). *Dialectical thinking and adult development.* Norwood, NJ: Ablex.

Basseches, M. (2005). The development of dialectical thinking as an approach to integration. *Integral Review, 1*, 47–63.

Bateson, G. (1979, 2000). *Steps to an ecology of mind: Collected essays in anthropology, psychiatry, evolution, and epistemology.* Chicago, IL: University of Chicago Press.

Baxter, L.A., & Montgomery, B.M. (1996). *Relating: Dialogues and dialectics.* New York, NY: Guilford Press.

Benack, S., Basseches, M., & Swan, T. (1989). Dialectical thinking and adult creativity. In J.A. Glover, R.R. Ronning, & C.R. Reynolds (Eds.), *Handbook of creativity* (pp. 199–208). New York, NY: Plenum.

Ben-Ari, A. (1995). Coming out: A dialectic of intimacy and privacy. *Families in Society: The Journal of Contemporary Human Services, 76*, 306–314.

Ben-Ari, A. (2012). Rethinking closeness and distance in intimate relationships: Are they really two opposites? *Journal of Family Issues, 33*, 389–410. doi:10.1177/0192513X11415357.

Ben-Ari, A., & Adler, A. (2010). Dialectics between splitting and integrating in the lives of heterosexually married gay men. *Psychology, 1*, 106–112.

20   *Maps, Territories, and the Ontological/Epistemological*

Ben-Ari, A., & Dayan, D. (2008). Splitting and integrating the enabling narratives of mental health professionals who lived with domestic and intimate violence. *Qualitative Inquiry, 14,* 1425–1443.

Ben-Ari, A., & Enosh, G. (2010). Processes of reflectivity: Knowledge construction in qualitative research. *Qualitative Social Work, 10,* 152–171. doi:10.1177/1473325010369024.

Enosh, G., & Ben-Ari, A. (2010). Cooperation and conflict in qualitative research: A dialectical approach to knowledge production. *Qualitative Health Research, 20,* 125–130. doi:10.1177/1049732309348503.

Friberg, F., & Öhlén, J. (2010). Reflective exploration of Beekman's participant experience. *Qualitative Health Research, 20,* 273–280. doi:10.1177/1049732309354988.

Montgomery, B.M., & Baxter, L.A. (Eds.). (1998). *Dialectical approaches to studying personal relationships.* Mahwah, NJ: Lawrence Erlbaum.

Rawlins, W.K. (1989). A dialectical analysis of the tensions, functions and strategic challenges of communication in young adult friendships. In J.A. Anderson (Ed.), *Communication yearbook 12* (pp. 157–189). Newbury, CA: Sage Publications.

Rawlins, W.K. (1992). *Friendship matters: Communication, dialectics, and the lifecourse.* New York, NY: Aldine de Gruyter.

von Glaserfeld, E. (1989). Cognition, construction of knowledge, and teaching. *Synthese, 80,* 121–140.

von Glasersfeld, E. (2013). *Radical constructivism.* London: Routledge.

Watzlawick, P., Weakland, J.H., & Fisch, R. (1974). *Change: Principles of problem formation and problem resolution.* New York, NY: WW Norton & Company.

Part Two

Personal Implications of Reflectivity, Researchers' Reflectivity, and Participants' Reflectivity

3 Reflectivity Reconsidered

This chapter focuses on the contribution of reflectivity to the epistemological stance vis-à-vis the phenomena under question. Its aim is to put forward the construct of reflectivity as a cornerstone of a research endeavor embodied in the qualitative paradigm. In previous chapters, we have dealt with the constructivist framework, and the dialectical perspective, which we consider a necessary outgrowth of the constructivist framework. Dialectical thinking is reflective in nature. It corresponds to what von Glaserfeld referred to as the higher level of knowledge construction, where one reflects on the process of scheme construction that emerges following the encounter with perturbations or apparent contradictions. As Ho (2000) described it:

> dialectical thinking emerges when one becomes aware of the manifold levels of complexity involved in human cognition, including one's own. Without such awareness, dialectical thinking remains an unrealized human potential. Dialectical thinking matures when the thinker systematically investigates the inter-relations among constituent parts and part-whole relations within the organizational structure of cognition. (p. 1065)

Becoming aware of one's thinking and ways of thinking regarding the phenomenon at hand is a reflective process, a turning of one's awareness upon itself, as Mead (1934) described it.

Reflectivity or reflexivity (Sandelowski & Barroso, 2002; Schon, 1983) has been described using several related terms, including reflection (e.g., Daudelin, 1996) and reflectivity (Ben-Ari & Enosh, 2011; Burns & Engdahl, 1998). These related terms are often used interchangeably in the literature (e.g., Gergen, 1999, 2001; Schon, 1983). Originally, 'Reflection' was defined by John Dewey as the

> active, persistent and careful consideration of any belief or supposed form of knowledge in light of the grounds that support

it and the further conclusions to which it tends [that] includes a conscious and voluntary effort to establish belief upon a firm basis of evidence and rationality. (1933, p. 9)

Following Dewey, we treat reflectivity as a deliberate awareness, involving both a *contemplative stance* and an *intentional activity* aimed at recognizing differentness and generating knowledge. In this sense, reflectivity is geared toward that which is implicit – not a given or self-evident. Thus, reflective processes simultaneously involve both a *state of mind* and *active engagement*.

The process of active engagement entails a movement of awareness both into and out of the phenomenon. The introduction of this constant movement between being **in** the phenomenon and stepping **outside** of it was presented by Daudelin who wrote about "the process of stepping back from an experience, to ponder . . . its meaning to the self through the development of inferences" (Daudelin, 1996, p. 39). Similarly, Enosh and Buchbinder (2005) have described the process by which interviewees relate to the phenomenon that they are being interviewed about by moving into and out of the experience. Taking a dialectic step and going beyond the dichotomy of individual and social, it should be noted that the reflective process may relate also to the ways by which researchers approach general social phenomena. Thus, experiencing the phenomenon from *within*, on the personal level is akin to what Pike (1954) referred to from a cultural level as the *emic* perspective, whereas experiencing the phenomenon from *outside* is akin to what he termed and *etic* perspective.

From this perspective, reflectivity may be thought of as involving active, conscious processes that emphasize the dual position of being both within and outside the phenomenon, requiring constant movement between the two. This position could be thought of as representing a "liminal space" between two different existential planes (Meyer & Land, 2005; Turner, 1967, 1995). The question that arises is how does this movement across the liminal space start? What is the origin of knowledge construction, of the epistemological act of reflection? Within our dialectical–constructivist framework, we conceive the origin of knowledge construction to be the recognition of a "difference that makes a difference" (Bateson, 1979, p. 99), or a "sense of differentness" (Enosh, Ben-Ari, & Buchbinder, 2008). A sense of differentness is equivalent to what von Glaserfeld (1989) has referred to as "perturbations." When one notices that existing schemes do not perform as expected, when one notices an apparent contradiction, and the need to reconcile this differentness overcomes the tendency to hold on to the "known" and trivialize the difference. Having said this, we can now move on to discuss the more practical aspects of reflectivity. Those aspects include four levels at which reflectivity may occur, as well as analytical procedures that facilitate the movement of awareness among those levels.

Levels of Analysis

The four levels of reflectivity we have identified (Ben-Ari & Enosh, 2011) that take place in the reflection process are: Observation, accounting, deliberation, and reconstruction. Moving from a lower to a higher level of analysis and contemplating previous knowledge from a higher inductive level are both complementary aspects of reflectivity. This activity may lead to a new way of understanding that transforms the meaning and perspective regarding previously acquired information. It is imperative to note that our conceptual model, with its four levels of analysis described below, should be considered as a heuristic instrument. The model is based on the movement between *being within* and *being outside* of the phenomenon (Enosh & Buchbinder, 2005).

Observation

Observation occurs at the initial (or renewed) encounter with the phenomenon. It is one of the earliest and most basic forms of gathering information and gaining knowledge, and is one of the main sources of gathering material about the social world (Adler & Adler, 1998). Observation involves making sense, considering meanings, making inferences, interpreting, and drawing conclusions (Patton, 2002).

As such, it may apply either to the researcher's first encounter with the phenomenon to be studied, with the context in which the study takes place, or with a particular participant. It also applies to the participants themselves, as they may reflect on their first encounter with the phenomenon (on which they are asked to reflect), or on the ways by which they experience it (Enosh & Buchbinder, 2005). Participants may reflect upon a known experience, which, until now they have taken for granted, and by reflecting discover or construct new aspects and nuances that present that phenomenon anew.

Accounting

When encountering a phenomenon, the observer (a researcher or participant) accounts for one's experience. This account takes the form of a narrative, a story of the phenomenon, of the encounter. This story goes beyond the initial observation, and develops an existence by, and of, itself. For researchers, such accounts may take the form of field notes, journaling, or telling oneself and others the story of the encounter. For participants, it may take the form of narrating the experience with the phenomenon to themselves and to others.

Thus, accounting in research refers to the process of understanding how both researchers and participants account for their experiences. Pike (1954) coined the terms "emic" and "etic" to denote the differences between the perspectives of insiders and outsiders to a phenomenon, respectively. It could have been claimed that participants' accounts present an emic perspective, whereas the researchers' accounts present an etic one. Yet, if we look at the researchers' experiences as the phenomenon at hand, their account presents their own emic experience. Therefore, at this level, the distinction between emic and etic perspectives appears to be the central focus of the analytical process. Researchers should be aware of the existence of both the insider's and the outsider's perspectives and be able to move between them and integrate them. The process then becomes a process of analysis and reflection. It is a process involving deliberate filtering and choice on the part of the researchers and, therefore, a process that tries to be true to the participants' narratives and interpretations, yet necessarily involves choice (implying interpretation) on the part of the researcher.

Deliberation

At this level, reflectivity moves officially from the emic to the etic by attempting to identify recurrent themes – experiential, behavioral, relational, linguistic, or other. Practically, "reflectors" are inductively engaged in an active process of creating meaning out of repetitive patterns in the accounts – whether their own or of others. These patterns can be represented as dimensions, categories, classification schemes, or themes. Once these representations have been constructed, it is often useful to cross-classify them in order to generate new insights about how the data may be organized and to look for patterns that may not have been immediately obvious in the initial analysis (Patton, 2002; Tesch, 1990). Such a process can lead to the identification of configurations of behaviors, relationships, and meanings, which can then be developed into a comprehensive conceptual model of the phenomenon at hand. Taking an active approach in order to look for new patterns through which to construct one's knowledge is the hallmark of our understanding of reflectivity.

Reconstruction

The fourth level of reflection is centered on integrating the knowledge produced at the previous levels by examining such knowledge within the wider context of the phenomenon. Being reflective involves self-questioning and self-understanding (Patton, 2002; Schwandt, 1997). Reflectivity in research requires an ongoing examination of the cultural, social, linguistic, and ideological context of the phenomenon at hand, as well as the perspectives and voices of participants, and the intricate relationships between all the parties involved (Enosh & Ben-Ari, 2010). Furthermore, it revolves around integrating all of the different perspectives, ideas, themes, and categorizations that emerged, into a coherent framework of understanding that may be presented as a "theory" or a coherent narrative of the phenomenon at hand.

Analytical Procedures

Both researchers and participants may shift among the different levels of reflectivity. While doing so, they may make use of various analytical procedures, either consciously or unintentionally. Those analytical procedures are dialectical in the sense that they are based on the assumption that apparent contradictions at one level may be integrated as a synthesis of the two opposing viewpoints at a higher level of conceptual analysis (Enosh & Ben-Ari, 2010). Adopting a dialectical framework assumes that what might appear as contradictions could be resolved by observation from a more comprehensive systemic perspective. That is, discrepancies and opposites found at one level of analysis may be reconciled at a higher level of conceptual integration. More specifically, we explore how the concept of dialectics can enhance our understanding of the dynamics taking place within and between each level of analysis (Hegel, 1807, 1969; Wallace, 2005). We identified several practical analytical procedures of reflectivity derived from a dialectical line of thinking.

Contrasts and Contradictions

Encountering a contrast or apparent contradiction may trigger one's sense of differentness. It challenges our existing knowledge and sparks our curiosity, promoting our attempts at reconciling the two opposing poles. Therefore, when we recognize contrasts and contradictions, we can ask ourselves if they may be constructed as opposing poles of one continuum. By setting the opposites as poles on a continuum, we facilitate a broader understanding of the phenomenon in question and avoid the bias of a one-sided perception of it. The identification of a continuum defined by two poles requires an explanation that may further enhance the production of knowledge.

Pre-Existing Expectations

Pre-existing expectations are a specific form of apparent contradiction, or "perturbation," as von Glasefeld described it. The term refers to the preconceptions that guide everyone who encounters a new phenomenon or revisits a known one. Pre-existing expectations are inherent in the human consciousness as we always approach the world from the plots that we have previously constructed. As Patton (2002), who reflected on his own experience as a researcher and program evaluator, wrote: "We would never have understood the program without personally experiencing it, since it bore little resemblance to our expectations, to what people had already told us, or to the official program description" (p. 262). In an earlier work (Ben-Ari & Enosh, 2011), we described our experience upon entering a prison setting that while from outside appeared as any other jail, with high walls, barbed wires, thorough check-ups, and so forth, upon entering we encountered a place that resembled more of a resort than a prison. Thus, when encountering a contrast between pre-existing expectations and the actual experience of reality, one encounters perturbations that may start the process of questioning the meaning of those discrepancies, and thereby generate new understandings that lead to a higher level of conceptual integration.

Epiphanies and Turning Points

Like pre-existing expectations, epiphanies are another form of a sense of differentness. They may be defined as existentially critical moments indicating pivotal events, or turning points, in the lives of individuals (Creswell, 1998; Denzin, 1989). Experiencing such a turning point may create a discrepancy that makes a difference in the narrated phenomenon, be it a life story, the story of a community or of a project. Identifying those events that create a contrast between life prior to, and life following, the epiphany or the turning point for individuals, families, groups, or societies, reflects an awareness of differentness and leads to the construction of new meanings or understandings.

Figure and Ground

Figure and ground is a concept drawn from the Gestalt tradition in the psychology of perception as a metaphor for higher cognitive processes (Thompson, Locander, & Pollio, 1989). This metaphor demonstrates that, upon encountering a phenomenon, researchers and participants have to focus on certain aspects of it (the figure), while letting other aspects fade into the background (Thompson et al., 1989). Figure and ground can then be reversed, as aspects that were previously in the background can come to the forefront, while those previously in focus can fade into the background. This yields a new picture with new information, which may be completely different from the one previously obtained. Shifting perspectives between figure and ground changes the way in which researchers may think about the phenomenon at hand, with the figure of one perspective providing an essential base for the other. This process implies that figure and ground cannot exist independently, since the ground is essential in defining the figure and vice versa (Thompson et al., 1989). By reflecting upon and accepting both figure and ground and their role-reversal, one fulfils the dialectical potential and transcends the either/or simplistic understanding of the phenomenon, thereby constructing a new way of understanding it.

The conceptual model integrating the four levels of reflection and the analytical procedures may be illustrated graphically using Figure 3.1. In the center of the figure are the four levels of analysis, with Observation at the bottom and Contextualization and Reconstruction at the top. Between the levels, one can find the analytical procedures of reflectivity, which facilitate the move from one level to the next. The point to emphasize here is that the same analytical procedures may be used in the movement between the four analytical levels of reflection. The arrows at the sides represent the directionality of the two parallel aspects of reflectivity.

Reflectivity as a Second Order Level of Knowledge Construction

In their classical book *Change: Principles of problem formation and resolution* Watzlawick, Weakland, and Fisch (1974) distinguished between first-order and second-order change, implying that change can be understood to occur at/on two levels. First-order change is bounded by the rules of the system, while second-order change is geared *towards* the rules of the system. Working within the frameworks of systemic and communication theory, they have claimed that first-order change relates to positively changing the individuals in a setting in an attempt to fix a problem. Second-order change refers to systems and structures involved with the problem. In dialectical terms, a second-order change synthesizes two opposing stances into a higher level of conceptual analysis. The synthesis itself becomes a new thesis, which in turn is negated by a new antithesis, thereby producing new synthesis in an endless process of knowledge production (Ben-Ari & Enosh, 2010; Enosh & Ben-Ari, 2010). Basseches (2005) who contributed significantly to the development of modern age dialectics defines dialectics as a second-order change, as a "movement through forms," which is in contrast to "movement within forms" (first-order change). We contend that "movement through forms" refers to the dialectical ability to view issues from multiple perspectives and arrive at the most reasonable reconciliation of seemingly contradictory information. *This is the essence of reflectivity.* It is a form of analytical reasoning that produces knowledge as long as there are questions, conflicts, and apparent contradictions, and the use of one's sense of differentness to notice those, and actively seeks to reconcile them at a higher level of integration.

References

Adler, P.A., & Adler, P. (1998). Observational techniques. In N.K. Denzin & Y.S. Lincoln (Eds.), *Collecting and interpreting qualitative materials* (pp. 79–109). Thousand Oaks, CA: Sage Publications.

Basseches, M. (2005). The development of dialectical thinking as an approach to integration. *Integral Review, 1*, 47–63.

Bateson, G. (1979, 2000). *Steps to an ecology of mind: Collected essays in anthropology, psychiatry, evolution, and epistemology.* Chicago, IL: University of Chicago Press.

Ben-Ari, A., & Enosh, G. (2011). Processes of reflectivity: Knowledge construction in qualitative research. *Qualitative Social Work, 10*, 152–171. doi:10.1177/1473325010369024.

Burns, T.R., & Engdahl, E. (1998). The social construction of consciousness: Part 2: Individual selves, self-awareness, and reflectivity. *Journal of Consciousness Studies, 5*, 166–184.

Creswell, J.W. (1998). *Qualitative inquiry and research design: Choosing among five traditions.* Thousand Oaks, CA: Sage Publications.

Daudelin, M.W. (1996). Learning from experience through reflection. *Organizational Dynamics, 24*, 36–48.

Denzin, N.K. (1989). *The research act.* Newbury Park, CA: Sage Publications.

Dewey, J. (1933). *How we think: A restatement of the relation of reflective thinking to the educative process.* Lexington, MA: Heath.

Enosh, G., & Ben-Ari, A. (2010). Cooperation and conflict in qualitative research: A dialectical approach to knowledge production. *Qualitative Health Research, 20*, 125–130. doi:10.1177/1049732309348503.

Enosh, G., Ben-Ari, A., & Buchbinder, E. (2008). Sense of differentness in the construction of knowledge. *Qualitative Inquiry, 14*, 450–465. doi:10.1177/1077800407311962.

Enosh, G., & Buchbinder, E. (2005). Strategies of distancing from emotional experience: Making memories of domestic violence. *Qualitative Social Work, 4*(1), 9–32.

Gergen, K.J. (1999). *An invitation to social construction.* London: Sage Publications.

Gergen, K.J. (2001). *Social construction in context.* London: Sage Publications.

Hegel, G.W.F. (1807, 1969). *The science of logic.* London: Allen & Unwin.

Ho, D.Y. (2000). Dialectical thinking: Neither Eastern nor Western. *American Psychologist, 55*(9), 1064–1065.

Mead, G.H. (1934). *Mind, self and society.* Chicago, IL: University of Chicago Press.

Meyer, J.H.F., & Land, R. (2005). Threshold concepts and troublesome knowledge (2): Epistemological considerations and a conceptual framework for teaching and learning. *Higher Education, 49*, 373–388.

Patton, M.Q. (2002). *Qualitative research and evaluation methods.* Thousand Oaks, CA: Sage Publications.

Pike, K. (1954). *Language in relation to a unified theory of the structure of human behavior* (Vol. 1). Glendale, CA: University of California, Summer Institute of Linguistics. Republished in 1967. The Hague, the Netherlands: Mouton.

Sandelowski, M., & Barroso, J. (2002). Finding the findings in qualitative studies. *Journal of Nursing Scholarship, 34*, 213–220.

Schon, D.A. (1983). *The reflective practitioner.* New York, NY: Basic Books.

Schwandt, T.A. (1997). *Qualitative inquiry: A dictionary of terms.* Thousand Oaks, CA: Sage Publications.

Tesch, R. (1990). *Qualitative research: Analysis types and software tools.* New York, NY: Falmer.

Thompson, C., Locander, W.B., & Pollio, H.R. (1989). Putting consumer experience back into consumer research: The philosophy and methods of existential-phenomenology. *Journal of Consumer Research, 16*, 133–146. Thousand Oaks, CA: Sage Publications.

Turner, V. W. (1967). Ritual, Anti-Structure and Religion: a discussion of Victor Turner's processual symbolic analysis. *Journal for the scientific study of religion, 30*(1), 1–25.

Turner, V.W. (1995). *The ritual process: Structure and anti-structure* (3rd ed.). New York, NY: Aldine de Gruyter.

von Glaserfeld, E. (1989). Cognition, construction of knowledge, and teaching. *Synthese, 80*, 121–140.

Wallace, R.M. (2005). *Hegel's philosophy of reality, freedom, and God.* New York, NY: Cambridge University Press.

Watzlawick, P., Weakland, J.H., & Fisch, R. (1974). *Change: Principles of problem formation and problem resolution.* New York, NY: WW Norton & Company.

4 Reflectivity and the Researchers' Perspective

This chapter highlights and appreciates the unique aspects of the researchers' contribution to the production of knowledge. We maintain that such a contribution is constantly enhanced by the application of reflectivity. Before we begin, an introductory remark is in order, one which sets the stage for the upcoming analysis. Within the framework of the research process, we have to recognize that reflectivity is not only within "the researcher domain." That is, reflectivity is not only a researcher's skill, tool, asset, or capability. Yet, we do claim that researchers can facilitate the introduction of reflectivity into the entire research process, by encouraging participants to become reflective and by shaping the research encounter to become a reflective exchange. In that respect, while we want to promote the notion that reflectivity is a relevant concept to all research partners and to the research process as a whole, we clearly value the unique contribution researchers might bring to the production of knowledge by promoting reflectivity.

Reflectivity constantly assesses the relations between knowledge and the ways of achieving knowledge (Calas & Smircich, 1992, p. 240). It can enhance researchers' competency both theoretically and experientially. If researchers are aware of the potential inherent in reflectivity to the production of new knowledge, they can create a difference in both the research process and its outcome. It is mainly because researchers appreciate the significance of reflectivity for the production of new knowledge. When applied to a researcher's perspective, reflectivity can be considered within two different, although related frameworks. We can think about researchers as *knowledge producers* and as *research partners* and examine how reflectivity is related to both.

Researchers' Reflectivity: Epistemological and Relational Perspectives

Science is a human activity (Maturana, 1991) and human activity is socially constructed (Berger & Luckman, 1966; Denzin & Lincoln, 2005; Gergen, 1985; Holstein & Gubrium, 2011). As qualitative researchers holding onto constructivist principles, and applying those to our own research, we believe that the research process itself is socially constructed with researchers *included in it*. Here is where a tensioned duality appears. The commitment to constructivist principles implies the inclusion of the researcher in the research situation being studied. The mere fact of studying a phenomenon in the socially constructed world requires some remote (detached) perspective. However, the fact that researchers are included in the research situations, the ones they are supposed to study may present some challenges to the very act of studying. In other words, how is it possible to be "in and out" of a certain phenomenon at the same time?

In order to understand one's position within the phenomena, the researcher also becomes the researched; turning one's awareness back on one's experiences (Mead, 1934). A similar idea was expressed by Maton (2003) who maintained that one of the most common forms of reflectivity in research is in the form of a brief autobiographical narrative of the researcher's own journey to the research. Here is where the significance of reflectivity emerges. Reflectivity enables being "in and out" of the studied phenomenon, simultaneously. This dual position of "in and out" not only defines researchers' role in the research endeavor, it also characterizes it as situated within a liminal space. How can reflectivity enhance researchers' performance as *knowledge producers* and as *research partners*? This question consists of two parts: epistemological and relational. The former confronts the relationship between reflectivity and the knowledge producer, that is, how reflectivity can enhance the production of knowledge. The later, the relational question, examines how reflectivity can contribute to research relations or partnerships.

Epistemological Considerations of Researchers' Reflectivity: A Knowledge Producer's Perspective

Researchers bring two types of knowledge to the research project: their academic, theoretical, and analytical knowledge of the phenomenon at hand ("know about"), as well as their abilities, skills, experience, and competencies in doing empirical research ("know-how"). We claim that reflectivity can improve both the "know about" and the "know-how" and, as a result, the knowledge produced out of that which is to be known. It can help bridge between the "research about" and the "research with," by helping researchers become more connected or involved in a more engaging research process.

Utilizing reflectivity in their creation of knowledge implies that researchers apply an outward view at the social and cultural artifacts and forms of thoughts that shape their lives and inward towards themselves to challenge the processes through which they make sense of their world. What is important is that researchers are aware of the liminal nature of their role since it becomes one of their most enabling and important tools. How can reflectivity improve their academic, theoretical, and empirical competencies? Reflective processes involve both a state of mind and an active engagement resulting in deliberate awareness (Ben Ari & Enosh, 2011). We can think of reflectivity as an intentional activity of adopting a contemplative stance aimed at recognizing differences that make a difference, which is the origin of new emerging knowledge (Enosh, Ben Ari, & Buchbinder, 2008). We maintain that if researchers are cognizant and actively seeking out a sense of differentness, then those perturbations in the analytical process of reflectivity as described in the previous chapter may lead to the emergence of new knowledge. Identifying and utilizing differentness is the researcher's responsibility. Such responsibility calls upon them to train themselves to become alert and tuned into such signs of differentness, which may be found both in the content and context aspects of the research process (e.g., the phenomenon at hand, the role of the participants, perception of reality, shared moral stances, etc.). Following constructivist assumptions and implied dialectical approach, Watzlawick and his associates (Watzlawick, Weakland, & Fisch, 1974) contributed to communication theory and family therapy by stressing that both the *content* and the *context* (*systemic*) aspects of communication (relational, modes of expression, systemic rules, etc.) are essential parts of the information transmitted, when referring to communication and meta-communication. We contextualize this distinction and use it to differentiate between the content conveyed in research interviews and the relational aspects, as the context within which the interview takes place. Along this line, we claim that processes of knowledge production need to consider both content and context as sources of new knowledge. As researchers, we focus both on what is being said or done by participants (content) and on the framework within which the communication takes place (context). Although researchers are intellectually aware of the significance of context as a source from which meanings and knowledge can be derived, many are practically inclined to analyze interviews based solely on the content dimension. By disregarding the context dimension, the relational, systemic aspects of the interviews and their significance to the production of knowledge are often left unutilized.

When things appear to be trivial or self-evident, no curiosity arises. There is neither a will nor a desire to explore, understand, or learn. When researchers find themselves in such situations, no research questions are being formulated in order to open up channels of exploration. Assuming a "taking for granted" attitude may lead to trivializing the phenomenon under study and block exploration and genuine curiosity and thus choke off the production of new knowledge. This results in triviality obstructing exploration and learning. A similar idea was expressed by White & Epston (2001), who emphasized the problematization of the-taken-for granted knowledge and day-to-day reasoning, as being barriers to the creation of knowledge. A sense of differentness contrasts, and is the opposite of, triviality. Researchers are likely to use exploration whenever they believe that the phenomenon under study is not trivial, nor self-evident. In order to utilize the potential inherent in this notion to the fullest, researchers should adopt a skeptical approach to what may appear as unproblematic. Assuming an attitude that takes nothing for granted and sustains a high level of genuine curiosity may result in the formulation of research questions that would open channels of explorations.

How can this be translated into practice? Reflectivity is geared toward the *implicit*, neither that which is given, nor the self-evident. In other words, one cannot be reflective of that which is trivial or self-explanatory. Researchers' reflectivity directs attention to the complex relationships between processes of knowledge production and the contexts within which such processes take place. This recognition is significant and applicable to both the content (what is being studied) and the process (how it is being studied). We maintain that it is the researcher's obligation, and to some extent responsibility, to be tuned into and able to identify these signs of differentness in both the phenomenon to be studied (what) and in how it is being studied (how).

In a fascinating account of a study seemingly gone wrong, Vitus (2008) describes her attempts to learn about the experiences of second-generation teenagers of Middle Eastern origin in Denmark. In interviewing the youth, she encountered what she (as researcher) experienced as resistance on the part of the participants, expressed through their avoidance of giving direct responses to her questions, changing contexts, and giving apparently irrelevant answers. When reflecting upon those responses, she recognizes that the resistance was neither meaningless nor antagonistic, but rather incorporated a clear response to her unstated and implicit assumptions. As a researcher, she defined the goal of the study as understanding the experiences of foreigners in Denmark; however, the participants were reacting to this unstated assumption by demonstrating that they did not define themselves as foreigners, but rather as "regular" Danish adolescents, who are not any different from other adolescents. Thus, she realized that, through her questioning, she had unintentionally, delivered a certain message that went answered through those "resistance" tactics. In her account, she demonstrates how reflective processes contribute to the construction of knowledge through "sensing differentness" in the content, as well as the context, of interactions.

In addition to their theoretical or academic knowledge, in many cases researchers learn about the phenomena through their interactions with the participants, so their access to the phenomena is *indirect*. In this sense, participants' *experiences* and their *communication* with the researcher serve as a prism through which the researcher learns about participants' direct *experiential* knowledge. In this sense, qualitative research can be regarded as interpretive activity that is driven by an interpreter (researcher) who contemplates other interpreters (participants). This two-layered structure of interpretations, which originates from two different sources, characterizes the unique nature of qualitative research. Reflectivity may refer to the interpretation of interpretation and the launching of critical exploration of one's own interpretation of empirical material – the studied phenomena as narrated and told by participants. Here again, being tuned into the implicit, that which is not self-evident, may generate new knowledge. For example, we can think of how participants narrate their experiences, but we can also contemplate how their narratives are being told to the researcher, as it is in the telling that makes the difference (Enosh & Buchbinder, 2005). Within this framework, what is being said and how it is being said can be used as sources for the production of knowledge (Vitus, 2008).

Relational Considerations of Researchers' Reflectivity: A Research Partner Perspective

We maintain that research relations are an important source of knowledge and researchers should treat them as such (Enosh & Ben-Ari, 2010). Following in the footsteps of Bourdieu (1993) we are interested in the relational positions and social space between actors (research partners). Each research partner is relationally located within a social space, determining his or her (partial) view of the activities and of the parties involved. We do see the production of knowledge as a relational activity that is sensitive to status and power differentials and embedded in the interpersonal arena. Thus, when considering the relational aspects of a researcher's role, reflectivity contributes by increasing one's awareness of such elements. Therefore, researchers should learn to appreciate the contribution of the research relationship not only as a source of knowledge but also as a facilitator of the process of knowledge construction. The interactions by which knowledge is constructed must also take into account the relations of power that constitute all such interactions (Foucault, 1980). Here we are moving from the personal to the inter-personal or social sphere in the creation of knowledge.

Within this framework the liminal nature of researchers' roles becomes apparent. Researchers are part and parcel of the research endeavor, yet they are outsiders to the researched phenomena. Even for researchers conducting some form of auto-ethnography, or researchers studying academic phenomenon they are part of, taking the role of researcher entails an etic position vis-à-vis the studies phenomenon. While liminality had been previously discussed regarding its role in the production of knowledge, here it is examined within a relational context involving at least one more human being, the participant. Reflectivity directs attention to research partners, researchers and participants alike, inward, towards the researcher as a person, as well as to the experiences of the participants. The very nature of the "turning-back of one's experience upon oneself" may refer to, and include, all relevant research partners. Thus, in much the same way as the research process involves multi-layered structures of interpretations; it may also involve complex structures of reflectivity. To fully accept the research process as socially constructed would mean that reflectivity shapes and contributes to the research relations.

Within this context, we adopt and contextualize the concept of relational reflectivity (Parton & O'Bryrne, 2000). Reflectivity can be relational when the knowledge constructed by researchers and participants about a phenomenon in which the latter take part, or about the lives of the participants, is openly shared and discussed within the research relationships. Relational reflectivity implies challenging a priori assumptions and knowledge about participants. This approach values local, concrete knowledge (Geertz, 1973) that has been co-constructed by both research parties within the research partnership.

Relational reflectivity can be described as a critical approach to the generation of knowledge involving both researchers and participants that operates "in the moment." When applying a relational approach to reflectivity in research, researchers attempt to bypass and obliterate the status differences between them and the participants. They are constantly engaged in processes of questioning, identifying different-ness, and challenging the explicit. It is likely that by recognizing the merits inherent in such discoveries, researchers encourage partici-pants to join them in taking such a journey.

References

Ben-Ari, A., & Enosh, G. (2011). Processes of reflectivity: Knowledge con-struction in qualitative research. *Qualitative Social Work*, *10*, 152–171. doi:10.1177/1473325010369024.

Berger, P.L., & Luckmann, T. (1966). *The social construction of reality: A treatise in the sociology of knowledge*. London: Penguin.

Bourdieu, P. (1993). *Sociology in question* (Vol. 18). London: Sage Publications.

Foucault, M. (1980). Power/knowledge: Selected interviews and other writ-ings, 1972–1977. New York: Pantheon.

Enosh, G., & Ben-Ari, A. (2010). Cooperation and conflict in qualitative research: A dialectical approach to knowledge production. *Qualitative Health Research*, *20*, 125–130. doi:10.1177/1049732309348503.

Enosh, G., Ben-Ari, A., & Buchbinder, E. (2008). Sense of differentness in the construction of knowledge. *Qualitative Inquiry*, *14*(3), 450–465.

Enosh, G., & Buchbinder, E. (2005). The interactive construction of nar-rative styles in sensitive interviews: The case of domestic violence research. *Qualitative Inquiry*, *11*(4), 588–617.

Geertz, C. (1973). *The interpretation of cultures* (Vol. 5019). New York, NY: Basic Books.

Gergen, K.J. (1985). The social constructionist movement in modern psy-chology. *American Psychologist*, *40*(3), 266.

Holstein, J.A., & Gubrium, J.F. (Eds.). (2011). *Varieties of narrative analysis*. Thousand Oaks, CA: Sage Publications.

Lincoln, N.K.D.Y.S., & Lincoln, Y.S. (2005). *The Sage handbook of qualita-tive research*. London: Sage Publications.

Maton, K. (2003). Reflexivity, relationism, & research: Pierre Bourdieu and the epistemic conditions of social scientific knowledge. *Space and Cul-ture*, *6*(1), 52–65.

Maturana, H.R., & Varela, F.J. (1991). *Autopoiesis and cognition: The reali-zation of the living* (Vol. 42). Berlin: Springer Science & Business Media.

Mead, G.H. (1934). *Mind, self and society* (Vol. 111). Chicago, IL: University of Chicago Press.

Parton, N., & O'Byrne, P. (2000). What do we mean by constructive social work. *Critical Social Work, 1*(2), 1–17.

Vitus, K. (2008). The agonistic approach: Reframing resistance in qualitative research. *Qualitative Inquiry, 14*(3), 466–488.

Watzlawick, P., Weakland, J.H., & Fisch, R. (1974). *Change: Principles of problem formation and problem resolution.* New York, NY: WW Norton & Company.

White, M., & Epston, D. (1989). Literate means to therapeutic ends. Dulwich Centre Publications.

5   Reflectivity and the
       Participants' Perspective

When taking part in research, participants are called upon to reflect upon their life experiences, the phenomena being studied, their worldviews, and so on. The mere involvement in the research process, joining a specific project, thinking about and answering interviewers' questions, all involve the adoption of a reflective stance vis-à-vis the phenomena in question. Yet, we believe that for the most part, the majority of participants are not "automatically" reflective. The researcher, being aware of the potential embedded in reflectivity as a source of new knowledge, conducts the research process in a way that could facilitate participant reflectivity. In certain circumstances, participants may also react to the invitation to engage in reflectivity by attempting to avoid certain aspects of reflectivity (oftentimes, because what they are asked to reflect upon is deterring). Therefore, any discussion of the process of participants' reflectivity should also include an attempt to describe avoidance techniques.

In order for a person to engage oneself in reflective work, there must be some distance placed between the "observer" and the "observed" that enables the taking of a contemplative stance vis-à-vis the phenomena or experience in question. The distance between the "observer" and the "observed" creates a liminal space wherein participants may step in and out of their own experiences. This process of stepping in and out of the experience, and reflecting upon the experience, has been thought to occur over a potential continuum, whereby on one end participants are so engrossed with reliving their own experiences that they are devoid of the ability to observe themselves and, thus, of reflectivity. At the other end of that continuum, you find participants who are so reluctant to get in touch and relive their experience, which they minimize or deny its existence altogether (Enosh & Buchbinder, 2005). The relative position of the observer on this continuum is dynamic in as much as one can get as close as possible to the situation while at the same time distancing oneself from the concrete realization of this situation. The reflecting participant is constantly moving back and forth between the experience and a contemplative stance, between the internal and external points of view. In a way, it is the ongoing movement between the emic and the etic, whereby the transition itself is a source of new emerging knowledge. We may define the points along this continuum as levels of abstraction and explanation, detailing the relative position of the observer in his or her constant movement within the liminal space. The two poles of total absorption on the one hand and total alienation from the experience on the other hand, define the two extreme situations, where reflectivity is not possible. Instead, our interest is with the processes taking place in between these two poles, distinguishing levels of reflection and describing meaning-making transitions among such levels.

Levels of Reflection

Experiential Immersion

The first level of reflection is descriptive in nature. The participants are immersed in the reconstructed and relived experience. When narrating and describing the experience, they tend to report it as if it was happening in the here and now. Participants' reflection at this level stays as close as possible to the concrete and sensual facts, to the point of (sometimes) reliving past experiences, or narrating the ongoing internal emotional and cognitive experiences they are going through while participating in the study. Thus, participants may use concrete descriptions, while utilizing present tense terms, as if the described experiences are happening at that exact moment. Reflection at this level is the most primal one, as it requires minimal sense-making or attribution of meaning.

Account Making

At this level, the participants depart from the immediate and direct descriptive experience (or do not engage in it at all) and, instead, are engaged in the observation and accounting for those experiences. At this level, the accounting process seems to situate the processes and occurrences within a knowledge framework that is seemingly known and understood by both participants and researchers, so that no further explanation is needed except for the use of the specific terms and concepts that are being used. Thus, participants may use terms and ideas that are taken from psychological theories but have enabled the cultural lore. For example, at a certain point, a participant may describe her state of mind as "hysteria," or explain her spouse's behavior as being the result of his "PTSD." Such accounts may not be derived solely from scientific or pseudo-scientific knowledge, but rather from any explanatory framework that the participant may adhere to, and implicitly believe in. Thus, participants may explain certain occurrences as a result of "jinx" or magical influences. The explanatory frameworks being used at this level are not explicit but, rather, implicit and are taken for granted by the participants, derived from their worldviews (Enosh, Eisikovits, & Gross, 2013), cultural paradigms, and folk psychology (Wundt, 1916).

Development and Deliberation

In specific contexts of research, participants are being approached at a stage of their own personal or professional development, at which point they already have engaged in extensive reflective work regarding their life, situations, professional experience, or other phenomenon for which they are being interviewed. In such contexts, the participants go beyond mere account making but, rather, present a developed theory or perspective regarding the phenomenon or experience. Such a fully or partially developed deliberation of the phenomenon at hand is rarely the product of one "burst" of "eureka" but rather the culmination of reflective processes the interviewee has gone through by which she or he has considered and reconsidered, debated with themselves and others, and reached a comprehensive model by which they can make sense of their world. While such levels of reflection may be perceived as developed and articulated, it may be obstructive to an awareness of other ways of understanding the phenomenon, or even as a way of avoiding an awareness of certain aspects of it. This leads us to the fourth level of reflection – reconstructing understanding.

Reconstructing

The fourth level of reflection that may be achieved by participants is when, through the introspective mode raised by the research project, they reach a novel, different, and reconstructed understanding and explication of the phenomenon or experience they have related to the researcher. Reaching such a level of reflection by the participants is rather exceptional, and rarely occurs. Still, if and when a participant is approaching the situation, experience, or phenomenon that one is engaged in, from a truly curious and open-minded interest, and is engaged in an exploratory dialogue with the researcher, new insights may emerge that shed a different light on previously known facts. At times, a new understanding is described in the literature as an "epiphany" (Denzin, 2009). What should be understood here is that such new understandings depict a new way of constructing one's knowledge, leading to a recontextualization and new paradigms of meaning.

Participants' Shifting Focus

As we have previously discussed, reflectivity in general, and participants' reflectivity in particular, may be thought of in terms of focusing (or unfocusing) one's awareness. Throughout the encounter between researcher and participant, the latter may respond favorably to the call to reflect upon a certain aspect or experience, or they may choose to change the focus of the exchange in the encounter by shifting to another topic. From the perspective of the researcher, such a maneuver may be experienced as avoiding reflection, whereas from the perspective of the participant, it might be so, or it might be a reflective process, albeit different from the one expected by the researcher. The ways in which researchers construct their understanding of such shifts can impact their ability to construct new knowledge from the results of the study. However, before we elaborate on the researcher's perspective vis-à-vis participant's shift of focus, let us first look at different ways that participants may shift the focus of their awareness in the process of interviewing. One should note that while, at times, such a shift may operate as a reflective stance by the participant, at other times it may well be a shift away from reflectivity.

Trivialization

Trivialization is an attempt to minimize the significance of the issues in questions. By perceiving events, occurrences, behaviors as non-important, avoiding their uniqueness or potential meanings, participants may achieve the opposite of "sense of differentness," and rather than noticing the difference that makes a difference, they may deter attention and defocus the awareness of such phenomena. During the interview process, such trivialization may be detected through the use of generalizations and dismissive maneuvers throughout the conversation. An example of this is saying "and we had an exchange of words" to describe an event that, if probed and elaborated upon, we may discover had included the use of shouting, insults, cursing, or even physical violence.

Ordinarization

Ordinarization is somewhat akin to trivialization. However, whereas the use of trivialization is characterized by shifting awareness through defocusing the uniqueness of an event, situation, behavior, or other phenomenon, the use of ordinarization is characterized by shifting awareness to other issues – ordinary daily events. Such a shift in focus tends to flatten the importance of the issues the researcher is attempting to understand. Thus, for example, a wife of a drug-addict may start talking about her issues with her young child and the problems she is experiencing with the kindergarten teacher, rather than speak about her handling of her husband's problems.

Comparisons

Comparisons serve as a basic form of thinking or reality construction and, as such, are very common to all interview-based research. Participants tend to engage in comparisons of persons, of events, of behaviors, and of times. Thus, in a study of client aggression towards social workers, a participating social worker may compare the way a client is behaving to the ways other clients have behaved and, through such a comparison, minimize or negate the importance or the meaning of the first client. Or a couple who live with constant squabbles and rifts may compare themselves to others they know who engage in physical violence, thus minimizing the importance and meaning of their own relations. Constructing a comparison puts the focus on the "other" that is absent. This "other" may be other people (or families, or groups or communities, or other human categories), other places, or other times. Thus, for example, participants may talk about how wonderful things were in the past, thereby shifting their focus away from talking about the present, or they may talk about their expectations or fears of the future, again shifting the focus away from the present. Obviously, when the focus of the research is on another point in time, talking about the present may serve as a shift of focus.

Focusing on the Non-Existent

Focusing on the non-existent is characterized by participants focusing their attention on what is missing rather than on what currently exists. For example, a woman who was asked about the way she and her husband manage their interpersonal conflicts may begin with a saying such as "well, we don't use violence." Such a shift in focus may lead participants to talk about events that do not occur, rather those that do occur. Focusing on the non-existent is, in a way, a type of comparison. A comparison that is not between specific persons, places, or times, but a complete shift of focus onto something that is only imagery. This often takes the form of using "if" sentences, such as "if only I had . . ." or "if one day . . .". By talking about different "ifs," participants are implicitly comparing persons, places, and times. However, by focusing on something that does not exist, they avoid the need to acknowledge, elaborate, or otherwise reflect upon what actually exists.

Researchers may regard such shifting of awareness as a lack of awareness or of reflectivity on part of the participants and may interpret those as denial and avoidance. However, such a shifting of focus may also serve as a source of new knowledge, if the researcher is prepared to make a shift in the way he or she understands and constructs the unsaid and possibly hidden meaning of these shifts. Thus, a reflective researcher would experience such shifts as being forms of communication and new knowledge emanating from the participants. Such construction of this emerging knowledge can lead to the understanding that participants are now merely avoiding reflectivity; they may be engaged in reflecting on what is meaningful and important to them, which may be quite different from what is meaningful and important to the researcher. Through exploration and active curiosity on his or her part, an active reflective researcher may help participants construct new meanings and generate new knowledge of their own experiences, resulting in shifts in awareness.

References

Denzin, N.K. (2009). Interpretive interactionism. *Encountering the Everyday: An Introduction to the Sociologies of the Unnoticed*, 397–421.

Enosh, G., & Buchbinder, E. (2005). Strategies of distancing from emotional experience: Making memories of domestic violence. *Qualitative Social Work*, 4(1), 9–32.

Enosh, G., Eisikovits, Z., & Gross, C. (2013). Between rigidity and chaos: Worldviews of partners experiencing intimate partner violence. *American Journal of Men's Health*, 7(5), 427–438.

Wundt, W. (1916). *Elements of folk psychology* (Authorized Translation by E. L. Schaub). New York, NY: G. Allen & Unwin, Macmillan Company.

6 Ethical Differences and Similarities as Sources of Reflection and Knowledge Construction

The research act is a meeting place between the researcher and the participants. In this meeting the interaction is affected by their status differences (Chapter 7), by issues of self-presentation and control of knowledge (Chapter 8), and, no less important, a meeting of moral worldviews that affect the stances each partner in the research endeavor takes vis-à-vis the phenomenon at hand, which often affect the identity formation of the participants.

Almost every social phenomenon is inherently value-laden, and qualitative researchers have been aware of this fact for many years, having emphasized the need for reflectivity regarding the researcher's assumptions, preconceptions, and moral attitudes. Yet, scant scholarly attention has been given to the moral stances of the participants, and to the effect the interaction between such moral stances may have on the process of knowledge construction. The moral stances of the participants and of the researchers can be analyzed and delineated in many extremely complicated ways that might warrant a book in itself. At this point, we would like to direct our attention to the extreme cases that might highlight the importance of the issue and its implications to the production of knowledge. For that purpose, we would like to focus on four potential configurations of moral stances of researchers and participants as sources of interaction, reflection, and knowledge construction. Real-life situations can never be neatly organized in a two-by-two matrix. However, for heuristic purposes of a clear presentation of our argument, we organized the analysis around the extreme points of two axes depicting the continuums between agreements and disagreements regarding the moral status of the phenomenon at hand, be it a behavior, a social interaction, or a defining facet of identity.

Positions of Agreement

At first glance, a situation in which both the interviewer and interviewee agree on the *positive moral status* of the phenomenon at hand,
and on the role played by the interviewee within this phenomenon,
may appear as a perfect situation – a meeting of minds that is the basis
for research cooperation and mutual exploration. However, this initial agreement may lead the research partners away from exploration,
stifling their ability to sense differentness (Enosh, Ben-Ari, & Buchbinder, 2008). When both the researcher and participant approach the
phenomenon at hand as being taken for granted, the dialog would
skim over it, and they would miss the opportunity to notice those
small misnomers, contradictions, incongruities, that could lead to
a deeper reflective process on both participants' and researchers'
sides. Put somewhat differently, in research situations characterized
by extensive agreement between interview partners concerning the
nature of reality, the limited curiosity results in a shallow exploration
that restricts or may even prevent the search for new knowledge.

Let us use the following interview excerpt as an example (quoted
from Enosh et al., 2008, p. 454):

I: Is there any tension between motherhood and lesbianism?

M: Why should there be any tension?

I: There might not be any.

M: I don't know. . . . No, the fact that I am a lesbian does not bother
       me. It has nothing to do with my daily experiences. That is,
       I share my life with a woman rather than a man, but I don't think
       it's different. Heterosexual couplehood is in no way different
       than homosexual couplehood.

I: Aha . . .

M: I don't think it is less difficult than any other type of couplehood.
       It is still a relationship between two people who love each other
       and want to connect and make something good out of it.

I: There is no contradiction.

M: No.

I: OK. Now, from a social stance, you mentioned before that you
       encountered some . . .

As this interview excerpt demonstrates, both interview partners
seem to minimize and/or trivialize the problematic aspects of the phenomenon, as both share the same value system regarding the relations between motherhood and lesbianism. As we can observe, this

"taken-for-granted" attitude in the treatment of the subject matter as a given or as self-evident is not only reflected in the use of words of agreement ("Aha," "OK," etc.) but also in the interviewer's early attempts to shift the focus of the interview to explore a different topic ("OK, from a social stance you mentioned before that . . ."). Such moves limit the possibility of sincere curiosity and/or deep exploration of the topic at hand and help bypass issues of power and control, social expectations, relationships with social environment, with family, and so on.

In the example we used, given the recent historical shift regarding social and moral perceptions of homosexuality, it is relatively easy to understand how the research partners could have looked for sources of differentness, not necessarily in their own moral perceptions but in other social interactions, and others' perceptions. However, their moral agreement regarding the normality of positivity of homosexual couplehood led them away from such exploration. However, as researchers, we encounter the same acceptance for taken for granted in so many other occurrences of qualitative research. Thus, we propose that putting a moral question mark in places we tend to take for granted, such as social roles and norms, may lead to richer research and the development of new understandings. Sometimes, adding such a question mark would entail a momentary adaptation of a moral position that is completely contrary to our profoundest beliefs. Such a move may be daunting; however, the purpose of the exercise is not to change one's moral standing, but rather to open up the possibility of a different understanding of the phenomenon at hand, and can lead to more genuine exploration and reflectivity.

Still, there is another form of agreement among researchers and participants that should be recognized. The second possible scenario concerns situations in which the interviewer perceives the nature of the phenomenon at hand as illegitimate rather than self-evident, and the interviewee is seen either as a "hero" or as a "victim." Such perceptions can generate a process of exploration that facilitates the construction of knowledge.

Take, for example, a story told by a social worker who was attacked with a pocket knife by a young female client (Enosh, Tzafrir, & Gur, 2013). She speaks about this young girl, whom she meets at a community center. The worker is the only one at the center with whom this young girl can actually connect. One morning, during an unofficial meeting, they sit and talk, and the young girl pulls out a small folding pocket knife and opens and closes it. Then, she suddenly asks, "and what if I cut you here and now?", and she does . . . .

During the interview both the social worker and the researcher share the horror of the moment, the appalling feeling of victimization and betrayal of faith. In their sharing the same reaction, they are similar to the interviewer–interviewee couple described above. However, unlike the previous example, the interviewer went on to explore the details of the occurrence and its outcomes, rather than staying at the abstract level of agreeing about the moral status of the behavior of the client. This led to the reflective process by the interviewee, relating to how, after the whole event was over, she had gone to the hospital to be treated, and had given her statement to the police. When she arrived home late at night, she started asking herself: "What did I do to deserve it? How did I trigger this attack?" This reflective recollection has eventually led to the development of the "disenchantment process of social workers" (Enosh et al., 2013), through the description and definition of the first stage of this process, the stage of "containment, forgiveness, and self-sacrifice." These reflective processes, both by the interviewee and by the researchers, could not have occurred without the interviewer's insistence not to fall prey to the befuddlement of mutual moral indignation in the face of client aggression.

Whereas agreement positions may enhance cooperation on the one hand, but may also deter deep exploration and reflectivity on the other, disagreements have the opposite effects. Disagreeing about the moral status of the behavior, occurrence, or persons, may more easily facilitate a sense of differentness; however, it may come at the price of the researcher inadvertently alienating the participants, and jeopardizing the research endeavor (Kadianaki, 2014; Råheim et al. 2016). Again, using our simplified scheme, we can say that such disagreements may arise in two different setups.

In the first disagreement option, the researcher considers the participants' behavior or their role in the social phenomenon as immoral. The participants on the other hand, perceive their behavior or role as normal, acceptable. The researcher's position can emerge through a variety of appearances, direct and indirect, verbal or non-verbal, through the way questions are phrased, by the tone of voice, or through straightforward declarations. The emergence of a disagreement of this sort almost automatically places researchers and participants into conflicting positions. The ways in which such conflicting positions may manifest, and the ways in which they may be handled. are the subject matter of our next chapters (Chapter 7 deals with status differentials, and Chapter 8 deals with issues of control over knowledge). However, it is important to note that the appearance of moral disagreement of this sort requires the researcher's the ability to "bracket"; to put aside one's belief system and worldviews, and be able to listen as openly as pos-sible to the ways in which the participants construct their world. Vari-ous researchers encounter such differences in different contexts. For us, this mainly arises when studying perpetrators of violence, which are extreme cases that almost everyone in Western culture would per-ceive as implying a moral wrong (e.g., Enosh et al., 2008). However, in the current context we would like to draw upon a completely dif-ferent context, a much more nuanced one, dealing with the conflict of identity definition, which eventually implies moral issues of belong-ingness, assimilation, and acceptance. Vitus (2008), in a fascinating description of her study of youth of Middle Eastern origin in Den-mark, describes how she experienced a resistance to her questioning expressed through apparently inexplicable changes of the discussion subject. For example, she would ask a teenager about his friends in the community center, and he would start talking about his favorite soccer team. Upon reflection, Vitus realizes that her questions had implied assumptions regarding the status of the interviewees. She automati-cally, through her definition of the research goals, and through her pre-set interview guide, had framed the identity of the boys interviewed as "foreigners," as "immigrants," although most, if not all, of them were born and raised in Denmark. Thus, the implied resistance to this fram-ing of their moral status is as not-belonging, as strangers, or outsiders. Their communicative tactics where directed at redefining themselves as local, belonging, part and parcel of the local and national society of Danish youth, and are no different from their school mates. In more extreme cases, such disparity between the researchers' construction of moral reality, and the participants' constructions, may lead to a com-plete negation and termination of the research project or, at least, of the participation of the specific person in the study.

The final alternative we present here is a situation in which the researcher considers the participants' behavior, or role, as normative and morally not problematic, whereas the interviewee is convinced that his or her conduct or identity is essentially immoral or wrong. Oftentimes, researchers in such situations perceive their role as going beyond data production and adopt an empowering role (e.g., Lather, 1988; Peled, Eisikovits, Enosh, &Winstok, 2000). Often, research-ers tend to oversee or misunderstand the participant's self-criticism or, adopting of such an empowering role, would try to "help" par-ticipants to change their "misperception." Thus, for example, Enosh, Ben-Ari, and Buchbinder (2008) describe an interview with a young ultra-orthodox male who is struggling with his homosexual sexual orientation. In this description, the interviewer, a Jewish secular male

researcher, although sympathetic to the interviewee's internal conflicts, seems to not fully comprehend the inherent contradictions in
the youth's situation, by not being part of the same cultural and value-
system, and cannot fully accept the participant's self-loathing. The
researcher is probing to understand the split between his belief system and the sexual desires that the interviewee is experiencing. The
conceptual differences in this case, between the psycho-theological
world of the interviewee and the modernized constructions of the
interviewer, serve as a source for exploration of differences and lead
to a reflective process by the interviewee and, later, to a deeper analysis and reflectivity by the interviewer.

Each of the interview partners attempt to use the interview to recre-
ate and preserve his or her worldviews by steering the course of the
interview according to the roadmap defined by his or her moral stance.
Such moral stances become an integral element in the constructed
knowledge that emerges from the interview. Every research project
serves as an arena that reflects the undercurrents of moral stances and
reality construction differentials existing between the research partners. Those undercurrents may be detrimental to the knowledge construction process by undermining the interview partners' motivation
to conduct an in-depth exploration of the issues at hand, but may also
be a motivating factor in the exploration of differences and, thus, the
source of knowledge production. Disagreements between researchers and participants regarding reality, nature, and moral status of the
participants, may be a source for misunderstanding and alienation.
However, when this possibility is taken into account by the researchers, it may serve as a significant source of sensing differentness and
exploring it by facilitating reflective processes by the participants and
by the researchers.

Watzlawick and his associates (Watzlawick, Weakland, & Fisch,
1974) contributed to communication theory and family therapy by
stressing both the content and the context (systemic) aspects of communication (relational, modes of expression, systemic rules, etc.)
as essential parts of the information transmitted, referring to them
as communication and meta-communication. We contextualize this
distinction and use it to differentiate between the content conveyed
in research interviews, and the relational aspects, the context within
which the interview takes place. Along this line, we claim that processes of knowledge production need to consider both content and
context as sources of new knowledge. While the content dimension
is idiosyncratic, by examining the contexts of research we may decipher common processes and underlying currents. Context serves as a

source from which meanings and knowledge can be derived, through examination of the relational aspects of the interview, as explicated in this chapter, and further developed in the next three chapters. By searching for differences that make a difference in the relational context, we may enhance the sources of knowledge construction beyond the content dimension.

References

Enosh, G., Ben-Ari, A., & Buchbinder, E. (2008). Sense of differentness in the construction of knowledge. *Qualitative Inquiry*, *14*(3), 450–465.

Enosh, G., Tzafrir, S.S., & Gur, A. (2013). Client aggression toward social workers and social services in Israel – A qualitative analysis. *Journal of Interpersonal Violence*, *28*(6), 1123–1142.

Kadianaki, I. (2014). Conceptualizing the mediating role of power asymmetries in research communication: A social representations approach. *Culture & Psychology*, *20*(3), 358–374.

Lather, P. (1988, January). Feminist perspectives on empowering research methodologies. In *Women's Studies International Forum* (Vol. 11, No. 6, pp. 569–581). Oxford: Pergamon.

Peled, E., Eisikovits, Z., Enosh, G., & Winstok, Z. (2000). Choice and empowerment for battered women who stay: Toward a constructivist model. *Social Work*, *45*(1), 9–25.

Råheim, M., Magnussen, L.H., Sekse, R.J.T., Lunde, Å., Jacobsen, T., & Blystad, A. (2016). Researcher-researched relationship in qualitative research: Shifts in positions and researcher vulnerability. *International Journal of Qualitative Studies on Health and Well-Being*, *11*(1), 30996.

Vitus, K. (2008). The agonistic approach: Reframing resistance in qualitative research. *Qualitative Inquiry*, *14*(3), 466–488.

Watzlawick, P., Weakland, J.H., & Fisch, R. (1974). *Change: Principles of problem formation and problem resolution.* New York, NY: WW Norton & Company.

Part Three

Relational Implications – Power Relationships, Power Differentials, and Reciprocity

7 Research Relations and Power Differentials

From Resistance to Collaboration and In-Between

In the previous three chapters we have focused on reflectivity as a main mechanism of knowledge construction. We have presented the construct of reflectivity and then differentiated between the researchers' reflectivity and participants' reflectivity. In the current and subsequent chapters, we plan to go beyond the individual parties in the research relations and discuss various facets of their interaction as sources of knowledge construction. We have adopted a reflective perspective, examining the interactions between researchers and participants, vis-à-vis the phenomena at hand, and have used it as an additional source for knowledge construction. In order to comprehend how this is possible, we should bear in mind that research contains both content and context dimensions. Although researchers may be intellectually conscious of the significance of context as a source from which meanings and knowledge can be derived, many tend to focus mainly on content and often disregard the context. By disregarding the context dimension, the relational aspects between researcher and participants (i.e., modes of communication, power differentials, moral stances, etc.) and their role in the research process would remain unconsidered. Interactions between individuals, including researchers and participants, consist of a set of exchanges where they attempt to make sense of, and interpret, theirs and their partners' verbal and nonverbal behavior within a certain framework of understanding. They often influence each other, or resist such attempts at influence; cooperate with each other, or obstruct each other.

In this chapter, we examine the influential role of power, social status, and hierarchy in shaping research relationships in qualitative research and how they relate to the processes of knowledge construction. Over/throughout the years, many scholars have addressed the gaps in social status and power between researchers and participants as detrimental to the research endeavor. Henceforth, we will discuss the nature of three interrelated concepts – power, social status, and hierarchy – and discuss how these concepts affect research relations, as well as the production of new knowledge, in different research settings.

Every study may be perceived as an arena reflecting the undercurrents of interaction, worldviews, moral stances, and status and power differentials between researchers and participants. Indeed, over the years, scholars in the field of qualitative research have bestowed special attention to the power/status differentials between researchers and participants (Karnieli-Miller, Strier, & Pessach, 2009; Vitus, 2008), to the ethical ramifications of those differences, and their implications for knowledge construction. Over the years, the gaps in social status, social positioning, and power differentials between researchers and participants has been emphasized by many scholars, and have been presented as being detrimental to the research endeavor (e.g., Edwards & Mauthner, 2002; Kvale, 1996, 2003, Holloway & Jefferson, 2000).

Thus, we now turn to discuss three related concepts that are essential to power differentials in research relations. We draw on Magee and Galinsky's (2008) conceptualization of hierarchy, power, and status that are extremely relevant to our analysis. The concepts of power, status, and hierarchy are often discussed in the qualitative research literature as being interchangeable (e.g., Karnieali-Miller, Strier, & Pesach, 2009). However, sociological research, especially that coming from the exchange theory (e.g., Thye, 2000; Magee & Galinsky, 2008), has shown that those concepts should be approached as differentiated and, at times, even unrelated concepts (Thye, 2000). Both status and power relate to the concepts of hierarchy and the exchange of values (Magee & Galinsky, 2008). The focus on status and power has begun with the work of Weber (1916, 1946), who related status to the social honor (value) attached to a group of people, to the work of Ridgeway and Walker (1995) who referred to status as one's standing within a social hierarchy as determined by the attribution of values such as respect or social influence. In human interactions, including research relations between researchers and participants, status characteristics serve as *interpersonal traits* that influence the beliefs individuals develop about each other's' capabilities (Thye, 2000). While status traits may be specific (such as athletic ability), those interpersonal traits are often diffused in the sense that they are acquired by belonging to a group that has attained a certain status in the general culture (e.g., race, gender, age, education, or occupation). Those traits give rise to generalized expectations for performance, which extend beyond the actual abilities of the person being considered. Such differences in performance expectations result in observable inequalities that impact the ways that the different parties to an interaction construct their perception of each other, their relative value, and the interaction outcomes.

Like status, power is a concept with a long history in sociological inquiry, and is commonly understood to be the ability to compel others to do what you want them to do, as well as the ability to manipulate others' thoughts or actions (Kelly, Burton, & Regan, 1994; Millen, 1997). Recent conceptualizations view power as a structural capability that promotes unequal resource distributions favoring some actors at the expense of others, or as having asymmetric control over valued resources in social relations (Keltner, Gruenfeld, & Anderson, 2003). Magee and Galinsky (2008) also agree that power is asymmetric since it captures the essential dependence between two or more parties involved in the exchange, where the low-power party is dependent upon the high-power party to either obtain rewards or to avoid being punished. In contrast, the high-power party is less dependent on the low-power party. Yet, to the extent that the low-power party can access resources, that is, has some control over the resources, the high-power party has less power. For example, a supervisor has control over his or her subordinate's career development, but the subordinate might have technical expertise upon which the supervisor is dependent. That is, the "formally" low-power party may now hold more power than their ranking would suggest (Mechanic, 1962). This idea is especially relevant to our analysis, as it will be further presented.

Research maintains that power may act to influence or bias people that possess it and thus suggests some attributes that are common to people in positions of power. For example, people in positions of power are likely to attend to information that confirms their beliefs (Copeland, 1994), stereotypes the powerless (Goodwin, Gubin, Fiske, & Yzerbyt, 2000), and distributes rewards in ways that favor their own powerful groups (Sachdev & Bourhis, 1985, 1991). To the extent that one's formal position provides control over resources that others care about, one has the power. Thus, the concept of power implies that there must be at least two individuals: somebody who has power and somebody over whom to have power (Dahl, 1957).

While power is defined in terms of control over resources, and the dependence of others on the provision of those resources by the power-holder, *social status* is defined in terms of respect or admiration by others (Magee & Galinsky, 2008; Ridgeway & Walker, 1995). Thus, differences in status are primarily based on subjective perceptions (Blau, 1964; Magee & Galinsky, 2008). Achieving social status is dependent on the subjective evaluation of the worthiness of individuals or groups. Individuals may achieve significant accomplishments; however, if those are not appreciated by others, their status will not be affected by their achievements. In other words, social status is based on the social construction of the worthiness of individuals and/or groups, and the subjective evaluation and interpretation of their value by other individuals within their group, or from other groups.

Both power and status constitute hierarchies. A hierarchy may be shaped by rules or by subjective understanding and create a rank ordering of individuals or groups according to a valued social dimension (Magee & Galinsky, 2008). Multiple valued dimensions may be in play in any given time; the importance, and relevance, of each dimension is determined according to the context. Thus, the very nature of power and status imply hierarchies, that is, power or status differentials.

At this point, we will examine the relevance of these three constructs within the context of research relations. A research project might focus either on the need to produce knowledge or on the needs of the target population. Whereas the goal of every researcher is the production of knowledge, the participants' goals are mostly defined by their personal and collective interests. It is clear that if the research focus is on the production of knowledge, the researchers and their needs are at the center, and the target population and other stakeholders are the means through which their goals are achieved. Conversely, if the research focus is on the needs of the target population, the researcher and stakeholders are nonessential. Since stakeholders are not, and cannot become, the focus of the study, their role is always secondary to the main research focus – be it knowledge production or the target population. The peripheral nature of their role might, under certain circumstances, create sources of antagonism and conflict between themselves and the research partners.

Scholars in various theoretical traditions of qualitative research have addressed issues of power relations. An element that is common to all those traditions is the notion that such relationships are primarily dichotomous, asymmetrical, and present the researcher in an unequal power relationship with the participant (Karnieli-Miller et al., 2009; Kvale, 2003; Limerick, Burgess-Limerick, & Grace, 1996; Reason, 1994). There are two main perspectives in regard to power differentials between researcher and participants (Enosh, Ben-Ari, & Buchbinder, 2008). The first views research relations as a symmetrical relationship between the research parties (Mishler, 1986). The second maintains that, in fact, research relations reflect an asymmetrical relationship, emphasizing inequality as a defining attribute of the exchange (Karnieli-Miller et al., 2009). The first approach might be perceived as attempting to achieve a utopist state of relationships, whereas the second one describes the actual reality of numerous research relationships.

Researchers, being in positions of power, may not be fully aware of how power differentials and potential abuses are viewed by the participants. The participants are able to recognize that power differentials can result in power abuses in certain situations within the context of research relations. Although researchers often trust themselves to be ethical in situations in which they have power, they may be biased or not see the potential abuse inherent in the relational research situation (Hoorens, 1995). They believe that they would act ethically in hypothetical situations. A major way of overcoming potential abuse of power by researchers is by adopting a reflective position, contemplating the social differences and situational context of the research relations. Furthermore, developing a dialog with participants regarding the power differentials and its potentially harmful ramifications to the production of knowledge may enrich the research project and enable co-construction of understandings, of the question under study.

Concerns about the abuse of power by researchers, as perceived by participants, may result in avoidance of participation in research. Often, participants may be reluctant to take part in research if they feel that they had been "used" by researchers in the past. From the perspective of the participants, usually there is less potential for the abuse of power. It is clear that power differentials can result in power abuses and may act to constrain people's abilities to behave properly in interpersonal interactions.

At times, differences in the social status between researchers and participants might get in the way of the joint endeavor of knowledge construction, since both research partners often come from different social backgrounds. From this perspective, the hierarchical gap between researchers and participants, where participants represent underprivileged social minority groups, may lead researchers to treat them in a stigmatized, degrading manner, looking at participants from a one-up to a one-down outlook, jeopardizing a genuine attempt to construct new knowledge.

In certain research contexts, when researchers are dealing with participants who belong to groups from a lower social status, the hierarchical gap may lead researchers to take a position in which they try to "solve" or "cure" the problem, thus diverting or shifting the focus from the main purpose of the research. This situation is similar to the therapeutic situation where the therapist is trying to solve the clients' problems rather than direct them to reflect upon their situation or the process in order to promote personal growth and development. The mere experience of solving social problems may get in the way of the generation of new knowledge. There are times where power differentials in research relations divert the focus of research in a way that perpetuates and reinforces such differences.

However, we suggest that paying attention to and contextualizing social differences as one of the ingredients of the research endeavor both shape and provide a new outlook and signify new directions for the production of knowledge. How can these conceptualizations be translated into real-life research situations? We would like to propose a simplified matrix that is comprised of two dimensions: Researchers and participants' perceptions of the hierarchy between themselves, thus, creating a typology of **four hypothetical categories.**

At this point, we would like to provide an illustration of those four categories: The first illustration presents a hierarchy where the researcher is perceived to come from a more advantaged situation, whereas the participants are perceived to come from a less advantageous situation, and the hierarchy is perceived as such by both. For example, let us look at a researcher who studies people living in poverty. This is the common situation to which many researchers have referred that raises the need to be ethically reflective and work on aspiring towards relationships of cooperation based on egalitarian research partnership. This prototype resulted in what today is mainly known as Participatory Action Research, which appreciates the contribution of the valuable information that participants bring with them to the joint process of knowledge production and diverts from the traditional perception of the participants as providers of information.

The second illustration presents a situation where the researcher perceives his or her status as coming from a more advantaged status, whereas the participants do not share such a perception of the status differentials. Let us consider a situation in which a researcher is embarking on a study of the "meaning and experiences of homelessness." The researchers perceive themselves as coming from a more advantaged social status to study the daily routines of people living on the streets, perceiving them as a disadvantaged group of people living in extreme poverty and deprivation. However, some homeless people experience their style of living as allowing for significant degrees of freedom, whereas they perceive the researchers as living in very restricted and rigid conditions. For them, the researcher comes from a system that restricts the basic freedoms that a human being should have. Thus, both research partners do not share the same view as to who has the greater advantage or disadvantage.

The third illustration presents a situation where each research partner perceives the other as coming from a more prestigious position. Let us look at a research situation where the researchers want to study experiences and meanings of burnout among a group of distinguished surgeons. While the researcher may perceive the surgeons as coming from a very respectful profession, the surgeon perceives the researchers as representing a desired academic affiliation.

The fourth illustration presents a situation where both researchers and participants perceive the status of the participants as higher than that of the researchers. Let us consider a research situation where the researchers want to study the marital relationships among highly-ranked, affluent hi-tech managers. Clearly, both research partners perceive the participants as coming from a significantly more advantageous social status.

The above illustrations suggest that the joint production of knowledge by researchers and participants needs to consider hierarchies, perceived or actual, as a significant ingredient of the knowledge produced, when taking into account the research relations between researchers and participants.

References

Blau, P.M. (1964). *Exchange and power in social life*. New York, NY: John Wiley & Sons.

Copeland, J.T. (1994). Prophecies of power: Motivational implications of social power for behavioral confirmation. *Journal of Personality and Social Psychology, 67*(2), 264.

Dahl, R. A. (1957). The concept of power. *Behavioral Science, 2*, 201–218.

Edwards, R., & Mauthner, M. (2002). Ethics and feminist research: Theory and practice. *Ethics in Qualitative Research*, 14–31.

Enosh, G., Ben-Ari, A., & Buchbinder, E. (2008). Sense of differentness in the construction of knowledge. *Qualitative Inquiry, 14*(3), 450–465.

Goodwin, S.A., Gubin, A., Fiske, S.T., & Yzerbyt, V.Y. (2000). Power can bias impression processes: Stereotyping subordinates by default and by design. *Group Processes & Intergroup Relations, 3*(3), 227–256.

Holloway, W., & Jefferson, T. (2000). Introduction: The need to do research differently. *Doing Qualitative Research: Free Association, Narrative and the Interview Method*, 1–6.

Hoorens, V. (1995). Self-favoring biases, self-presentation, and the self-other asymmetry in social comparison. *Journal of Personality, 63*(4), 793–817.

Karnieli-Miller, O., Strier, R., & Pessach, L. (2009). Power relations in qualitative research. *Qualitative Health Research, 19*(2), 279–289.

Kelly, L., Burton, S., & Regan, L. (1994). Researching women's lives or studying women's oppression? Reflections on what constitutes feminist research. In M. Maynard & J. Purvis (Eds.), *Researching women's lives from a feminist perspective* (pp. 27–48). London: Taylor & Francis.

Keltner, D., Gruenfeld, D.H., & Anderson, C. (2003). Power, approach, and inhibition. *Psychological Review, 110*(2), 265.

Kvale, S. (1996). *InterViews: An introduction to qualitative research interviewing.* Thousand Oaks, CA: Sage Publications.

Kvale, S. (2003, August). *Dialogical interview research – Emancipatory or oppressive?* Keynote speech given at the 22nd meeting of the International Human Science Research Conference. Stockholm, Sweden.

Limerick, B., Burgess-Limerick, T., & Grace, M. (1996). The politics of interviewing: Power relations and accepting the gift. *Qualitative Studies in Education, 9*, 449–460. doi:10.1080/0951839960090406.

Magee, J.C., & Galinsky, A.D. (2008). 8 Social hierarchy: The self-reinforcing nature of power and status. *Academy of Management Annals, 2*(1), 351–398.

Mechanic, D. (1962). Participants in Complex Organizations. *Administrative Science Quarterly, 7*(3), 349–364.

Mishler, E.G. (1986). *Research interviewing: Context and narrative.* Cambridge, MA: Harvard University Press.

Reason, P. (1994). Three approaches to participative inquiry. In P. Reason (Ed.), *Participation in human inquiry* (pp. 82–98). London: Sage Publications.

Ridgeway, C.L., & Walker, H.A. (1995). Status structures. *Sociological Perspectives on Social Psychology, 281*, 310.

Sachdev, I., & Bourhis, R.Y. (1985). Social categorization and power differentials in group relations. *European Journal of Social Psychology, 15*(4), 415–434.

Sachdev, I., & Bourhis, R.Y. (1991). Power and status differentials in minority and majority group relations. *European Journal of Social Psychology, 21*(1), 1–24.

Thye, S.R. (2000). A status value theory of power in exchange relations. *American Sociological Review*, 407–432.

Vitus, K. (2008). The agonistic approach: Reframing resistance in qualitative research. *Qualitative Inquiry, 14*(3), 466–488.

Weber, M. (1916, 1946). *From Max Weber: Essays in sociology* (Trans and Ed. H.H. Gerth & C.W. Mills). New York, NY: Oxford University Press.

8 Frames of Reference and the Control of Knowledge

Like in our two previous chapters, we would like to continue the analysis of research relations. Whereas in Chapter 6 we discussed agreements and disagreements between research partners regarding the moral status of the phenomenon in question, as well as issues related to participants' identity, and in Chapter 7 we discussed issues of status differentials as power positions, in this chapter we would like to take those issues one step further. We discuss power relations as those related to agreements and disagreements over the construction of reality, morality, identities, research agendas, and research relations. We would like to conduct this discussion through an understanding of the processes that take place when researchers and participants dialog, negotiate, or struggle with each other explicitly or implicitly, over the content and context of the ongoing research.

Traditionally, the researcher was considered to be a neutral/ passive observer of the participant's subjective experiences and a facilitator who helps the participants to unfold their fully developed narrative in their own terms. Thus, the researcher's goal was defined as not interfering with the participants' subjectivity. The objective of the research in general, and the interview in particular, was to achieve the interviewee's subjective truth (Douglas, 1985; Kvale, 1996). However, this passive perspective has led to criticism by scholars (e.g., Holstein & Gubrium, 2002) who have claimed that the researcher has an active role in the research process in general and the interview process in particular. As opposed to the passive interviewer/subject relationship, this approach perceives both parties in the interview as necessarily and unavoidably "active" in meaning making, constructing a version of reality through their interaction. This approach reflects a growing awareness that the research is a relational and interactional act (Josselson, 2013), one that motivates and shapes the dynamics of interaction between researchers and participants. From this perspective,

the researcher and the participants are treated as conversational partners, who monitor and affect each other's speech events or activities.
Accepting the fact that the research in general, and the interview in
particular, are interactive processes, in which both knowledge and
meanings are generated, raises questions regarding the power relationships between researchers and participants.

We suggest that common perceptions of research interactions
as either "positive," "collaborative," and "good," or as "negative,"
"antagonistic," and "bad" construct a misleading or false dichotomy. Adopting a dialectical approach to examine such relationships
between research partners we assume that apparent contradictions at
one level might, in fact, be integrated as a synthesis of the two opposing viewpoints, at a higher level of conceptual analysis (see Chapter 2). Interactions between researchers and participants consist of
sets of exchanges in which each partner attempts to make sense and
interpret the verbal and nonverbal behavior (of him/herself and the
other) within his or her "frame" of understanding (Goffman, 1974).
"Frame," in this regard, is defined as reflecting structures of expectations of the interaction partners (Bateson, 1972, 2000; Goffman,
1974; Tannen, 1993; Tannen & Wallat, 1987). Thus, we should perceive interviews not necessarily as shared and agreed-upon meaning-
making endeavors but, rather, as ambiguously complex processes
with multiple levels of "differences interrupting differences" (Scheurich, 1995, p. 243). In effect, both partners in qualitative research ask
themselves "Who am I in this encounter?" or, even more importantly,
"How do I define my place or position as the author and interpreter of
the phenomena in question within this encounter?"

The self, unique as it may be, is primarily realized through interactions with others, who in turn serve as the source of knowledge about
oneself (Mead, 1934). Appreciating and working with subjectivity
opens the door to true intersubjectivity. The interaction of subjectivi-
ties of both interview partners becomes the central axis around which
every research project turns. Each interview becomes an arena where
interviewer and interviewee negotiate the implicit question of "What
are the moral and identity implications of what is being said here *for
me?*" This implicit question leads them to address issues such as "What
should we define here as *important*, and what should we *overlook?*"
"Who is leading this interview and in what direction?" and "What
meaning will we develop for the agreed-upon construction of reality?" This is particularly true of interviews concerning sensitive issues
because, when dealing with such issues, differences may arise between
interview partners, concerning social status, moral values, identities,

and perceptions of the subject matter. In the past, scholars of qualitative research have cautioned against such differences, and interviewers were instructed to be prudent and prevent their own values and perspectives from influencing the interview process (Bogdan & Taylor, 1975; Bogdan & Biklen, 1982; Patton, 2002). However, we argue that the idea of a neutral interviewer, or even bracketing the interviewer's beliefs, is doomed to fail. Rather, paying attention to, reflecting, and using differences between the interviewer and the interviewee may prove to be the cornerstone for understanding the substance and process of knowledge construction.

Another cautionary note that often is brought up by qualitative researchers is against the asymmetric power relations, derived from either the status of the researcher or from the mere fact that the researcher designs the study agenda (e.g., Karnieli-Miller, Strier, & Pessach, 2009; Kvale, 2006). In this sense, Kvale (2003, 2006) presents the most extreme and cautionary voice, using the metaphor of the "gentle and enticing wolf" in *Little Red Riding Hood* (Grimm & Grimm, 2004) to warn participants against ill-intentioned researchers, and warning researchers not to abuse their power over participants:

> There are many kinds of wolves. Today, we could perhaps include some interviewers who, through their gentle, warm, and caring approaches, may efficiently circumvent the interviewee's defences to strangers and invade their private worlds. Their big eyes and ears sensitively grasp for potential consumption what the multiple interview voices tell them. (Kvale, 2006, p. 498)

However, when one reconsiders the details of this famous fairy tale, it may be claimed that, in its wholeness, it represents the intricacy of research relations in a much more complicated and nuanced way than attributed to it by Kvale. The story begins with the wolf indeed being the interviewer, gaining knowledge from Little Red Riding Hood as to her goal (going to grandma), behavior (wandering through the forest looking for nice flowers, etc.), and agenda (bringing old grandma food and other necessities). Indeed, later on, the wolf uses this knowledge aggressively in order to fulfil his own agenda (eating grandma and Red). However, in the meantime, there is a shift in roles, and when the wolf is in bed masquerading as grandma, Red becomes the interviewer wondering about the incongruities she finds between her everyday expectations and the reality she faces (too big eyes, too big ears, etc.). Her sense of differentness develops in order for her to gain a better understanding of the reality she is facing.

Those shifts in the plot are much more reflective of the turns and shifts of the "plot" in the research process. From our perspective, the main theme of this fairy tale is that control over knowledge shifts the foci of power between researcher and participant in unexpected ways that twist and turn the plot. Therefore, we argue that, from this perspective, power is constructed discursively, whereby each participant attempts to steer the research project but is simultaneously steered by the other. Given that the major goal of the research endeavor is the production of knowledge, power relations in qualitative research might be conceived as the power to impact the process and outcomes of knowledge construction (Enosh & Buchbinder, 2005).

Research may be divided into many phases. The major phase, at which most interactions between researchers and participants occur, is data collection, consisting mostly of interviews and/or observation. During this phase, the participants hold the knowledge of their experiences, while the researcher holds the knowledge about the conduct of research and, in so doing, attempts to promote the official research agenda. We argue that, at this stage, contrary to the claims presented above regarding the abuse of power by the researcher, the participants hold major anchors of power that they may or may not use during the process. The first such anchor is their participation. As long as no coercion to participate is involved, participants may, at any point, withdraw their participation in the research with no further obligations. The researchers are dependent on participants' cooperation to fulfil the data-gathering process, which gives such enormous power to the participants. Furthermore, we claim that the mere fact that participants have access to, and control of, the experiential knowledge for which they are being interviewed or observed shapes and defines the nature of their relationships with the researchers, whether they are aware of it or not. They may refuse to participate, negotiate the level of their participation, and/or negotiate the emerging meanings of discourse that is developing through the data-collection process, be it in an interview or through observation. Furthermore, at this crucial stage of data gathering, the question arises as to who produces the knowledge. Thus, in the course of interviewing there may be collaborative production, as well as a negotiation over facts, construction of myths, labelling, and interpretations. We can describe the interaction between researchers and participants as a continuum, ranging between a fully cooperative process, characterized by attempted reflectivity by the participants, to a fully antagonistic interaction, characterized by conflict and alienation. For analytical considerations, we can delineate five interaction styles along this continuum: (1) full cooperation,

(2) negotiation over reality construction, (3) deflection and power games, (4) discrepancies between declared agreements and actual participation in research, and (5) overt refusal or conflict. Moreover, we claim that although such interactive styles can be understood as reflecting power relations between researchers and participants, at the same time they may be treated as sources of new knowledge. We illustrate these interactive styles, using examples from previous and ongoing research projects.

Full Cooperation

The interaction between research partners might be characterized as full cooperation if both partners share the same moral values and convictions, social commitments, and intellectual curiosity. This shared point of departure would normally lead to participants' (or other stakeholders in the research project) agreement to be involved in the research endeavor. As discussed in a previous chapter (Chapter 6), agreement between researchers and participants may lead to reflective processes and further construction of knowledge. However, both research partners should be cautious not to let their agreements lead them into trivialization and the overlooking of apparent incongruities, contradictions, and surprises that may serve as points of departure for the construction of new understandings.

Negotiation

Often, researchers' and participants' perceptions of the phenomenon to be studied, as well as the research partners' roles, might not be fully in harmony. When participants or other stakeholders feel that the research project might threaten their interests, values, or identity, they might bargain over the process and outcomes of knowledge production in order to create a narrative that would coincide with their perception of reality. Thus, they might attempt to negotiate expectations, definitions of reality, or the meanings of the co-constructed realities. For example, Enosh and colleagues (2008) analyzed a research interview with a male batterer in which the researcher defined the interviewee's behavior as "violent," whereas the interviewee perceived himself as "normative." They demonstrated the negotiation process that took place, leading to a shared definition of the interviewee's behavior as "hand-raising" rather than stigmatically defining it as "violent." The process of creating a shared definition of reality and reconstructing mutual understandings is inherent in most research relationships. An awareness of such processes and attempting to comprehend the potential in furthering research goals through such dynamics might enhance both the production of knowledge as well as the enhancement of the target population's well-being.

Deflection and Power Games

The disagreement between researcher and research participants over the definition of reality can lead to deflective communication strategies in which researchers attempt to navigate the interaction around their perception of reality, whereas participants' responses might seem to be unrelated. Whereas in the previous example the participant reacts directly to the researcher's proposed definitions by suggesting alternatives, here the participants seem to ignore the researcher's questions or redirect answers to different topics. In this regard, Vitus (2008) exemplified deflective interaction between researcher and participants and defined it as *agonism*. Her vivid description includes an account of her research into the way minority adolescents of Middle Eastern origin experienced their "being" in Denmark. From her (the researcher's) initial perspective, the goal of the study was to study the experiences of being a stranger or an immigrant. Yet, when asking questions based on this framing of the research question, she ran into what she experienced as side-tracking and aversive responses. Thus, she describes how one adolescent repeatedly ignored her questions about "being different" by changing the subject to seemingly irrelevant issues, such as his favorite soccer team, his school friends, and so forth. Following a process of reflecting on these "resistances," she realized that the adolescent was trying to convey his *normalcy* (rather than his difference) by appearing like any other Dane.

To summarize, a deflective communication style may appear when researchers attempt to navigate the interaction based on their own perception of reality and the participants respond by navigating away. Participants' responses might appear unrelated, answering unasked questions, or evading questions that are being asked. Paying attention to such processes might help the researcher reframe and understand the interaction as a form of communication, thus enhancing the knowledge construction process and helping increase the understanding of the target population's needs and experiences.

Noncompliance

Noncompliance occurs when the researcher encounters a discrepancy between the declared agreement of the participants and/or stakeholders and their actual participation in the research. It might take two different forms: Either the participants are reluctant to fulfil previously agreed upon assignments or the participants attempt to mask information and/or previously discussed conventions. The researcher might perceive such behavior as resistance. The participants, however, might perceive the researchers as an external interference, and a threat to carrying out their own agendas, or as a threat to the continuance of the current state of affairs. When referring to noncompliance on the part of participants or stakeholders, we can detect a pattern of conduct, starting with a declared agreement to participate, followed by actual noncompliance (either by refusing to continue with assignments, or refusing to engage in providing information). Noncompliance is often characterized by justifications, accusations, and blaming (either the researcher or some third party). Thus, for example, evaluation studies create situations in which program managers (stakeholders) outwardly express enthusiasm and a willingness to participate in the evaluation. However, in spite of their outward enthusiasm, the same program managers might avoid the actual distribution of questionnaires to program participants, and fail to respond to any attempts at communication (Enosh, 2008). For example, in one evaluation study we encountered agency managers who repeatedly declared their enthusiasm for the research evaluation yet maintained behavioral reluctance, to the degree that delayed access for months. Such situations can be frustrating for the researchers, as they seem to lead to a dead end. As researchers, we might infer that the stakeholders or participants feel threatened, either consciously or unconsciously, by the research project. They might sense a danger to their immediate interests (putting the agency's funding or their jobs in jeopardy) or, on a deeper level, putting their professional abilities, credentials, or professional and personal identities into question. Experience indicates that initiating an open dialog, based on attempts to encourage reflective processes on both sides, understanding the needs, goals, concerns, and sometimes undefined epistemological and moral stances of both sides, may facilitate a meaningful change in attitudes, while enriching and contributing to the process of knowledge construction vis-à-vis the researched phenomena.

Overt Refusal or Conflict

For researchers, the most difficult and frustrating participant behavior is an overt refusal to take part in the research process. Sometimes, engaging in a dialog (as recommended above) may lead to a change in the position of the participants or stakeholders. However, this may not always be the case. In such situations, researchers might view abandoning these particular respondents, or even the entire project, as a viable option. However, it is preferable to consider other alternatives. For example, a study examining emotional transmission between spouses where one partner serves in an emergency unit that deals with terror attacks (e.g., police, paramedics, social workers) was approved by a national fund. The research proposal specified three groups of participants, based on the initial consent of formal representatives from each unit, and the researcher received the funds. After a lengthy negotiation process (15 months) with research officers from one unit regarding starting data collection (including presenting the research proposal, sharing preliminary findings, and promising to supply the unit with the findings), the unit officially informed the researchers that it had retracted its consent. The researchers informed the fund, who then decided to withdraw its assistance on the grounds of the researchers' inability to carry out the initially approved research plan. At this point, the researchers considered cancelling the entire project. However, they applied an alternative approach: They reconsidered the project's focus, identified an additional emergency unit, and consequently, were able to go ahead with the project.

All five interactive styles emerge from an inherent power differential – the participants control the initial access to the phenomenon that researchers would like to study. Other stakeholders hold the keys to various stages of the research process (funding, gatekeeping, ethical approval, etc.). From this vantage point, the researcher finds oneself in the less powerful position. The obvious question is: How should researchers react to these hardships? The shift in research focus from producing knowledge to considering participants' needs might lead researchers to avoid confrontation by either abandoning the research or ignoring the existence of resistive maneuvers. However, the approach offered here is to rethink and reframe all such occurrences as opportunities for knowledge production, emphasizing modes of interaction as a source of knowledge, which is the relational (context) aspect of the research endeavor. We advocate adopting a reflective perspective towards different forms of interactions and use it as an additional source for knowledge construction. In particular, we suggest that situations in which research participants are reluctant to take part in the process might be perceived as reflecting previously unknown interests, agendas, goals, and objectives, and thus might be used to expand our understanding of the phenomenon in question.

The main argument underlying our analysis of interaction styles is that all interaction styles might be contextualized as modes of communication, bringing the researcher to a second-order level of understanding (Watzlawick, Weakland, & Fisch, 1974; Watzlawick, Beavin-Bavelas, & Jackson, 1983) and, as such, serving as a source for knowledge. From an epistemological perspective, the researchers are called upon to further change their understanding and reframe all interaction styles as modes of communication. Taking a dialectical approach encourages the researchers to transform modes of resistance into a source of knowledge production. Instead of taking resistance, non-cooperation, and antagonism at face value, the researchers might regard these forms of interaction as a means of communication between themselves and the participants or stakeholders. Furthermore, the researchers might refrain from labelling their behavior as "good" or "bad" and from defining possible remedies as necessarily "good" or "bad." The initial task is to try to understand the communication at hand. What are the participants or stakeholders trying to tell us? Why do they adopt certain modes of communication as opposed to others? How do participants' modes of communication contribute to the understanding of the phenomenon? All of these questions are targeted at expanding the knowledge about the phenomenon under study. By asking such questions, the researchers link their relationships with the participants to the knowledge-production process. Recognizing the different interaction styles as modes of communication also helps the researcher create second-order meanings, resulting in a broader and more comprehensive understanding of the phenomenon. Moreover, adopting the approach that all interactive styles are, in fact, modes of communication can further provide the researchers with a deeper understanding of the needs of the target population and facilitate deeper reflective processes on both sides. Thus, resistance is not always bad and, therefore, should not be reconciled immediately, as it might serve as a valuable source of knowledge that would otherwise be unavailable. A second core theme that is implicit in the discussion, so far, is based on the claim that the goal of every research endeavor is to ultimately serve the interests of one or more of the parties involved. Researchers should contemplate the main goal and focus of the study. Is the study's aim to satisfy the researcher's need for knowledge? Is it to help the target population or to serve the interests of the stakeholders? When the target population is the focus of the study, researchers might not have the privilege of abandoning the research when encountering resistance or conflict but might be required to find a way of making the study viable. When dealing with an uncooperative program manager, the ultimate goal of the study is not the manager and his/her needs and interests; both he/she and the researcher are there to serve the target population. Who comprises the target population? Is this something that needs to be decided a priori or can it change throughout the process? These questions open up new avenues for exploration, rather than requiring definite answers. However, the question of whose interests are to be served might prove complicated at times as it involves a moral decision. This question is crucial, since the answer might call for the prioritization of the interests of one group over another. This leads to an even more pivotal question: Who is to decipher the interests of the parties involved in a research project? In other words, what is the actual focus of the research? Those questions remain for each researcher to work out with oneself, their colleagues, and with other research stakeholders – participants, gatekeepers, ethical review boards, and any other relevant parties.

References

Bateson, G. (1972, 2000). *Steps to an ecology of mind: Collected essays in anthropology, psychiatry, evolution, and epistemology*. Chicago, IL: University of Chicago Press.

Bogdan, R., & Biklen, K.S. (1982). *Qualitative research for education: An introduction to theory and methods*. Boston, MA: Allyn & Bacon.

Bogdan, R., & Taylor, S. (1975). *Introducing to qualitative methods: Phenomenological*. New York, NY: A Wiley Interscience Publication.

Douglas, J. D. (1985). *Creative interviewing*. Thousand Oaks, CA: Sage.

Enosh, G. (2008). Resistance to evaluation in batterers' programs in Israel. *Children and Youth Services Review, 30*(6), 647–653.

Enosh, G., Ben-Ari, A., & Buchbinder, E. (2008). Sense of differentness in the construction of knowledge. *Qualitative Inquiry, 14*, 450–465. doi:10.1177/1077800407311962.

Enosh, G., & Buchbinder, E. (2005). Strategies of distancing from emotional experience: Making memories of domestic violence. *Qualitative Social Work, 4*(1), 9–32.

Goffman, E. (1974). *Frame analysis: An essay on the organization of experience*. Cambridge, MA: Harvard University Press.

Grimm, J., & Grimm, W. (2004). Little red riding hood. In M. Tatar (Ed.), *The annotated Brothers Grimm* (pp. 140–149). London: WW Norton & Company.

Gubrium, J.F., & Holstein, J.A. (2002). *Handbook of interview research: Context and method*. Thousand Oaks, CA: Sage Publications.

Josselson, R. (2013). *Interviewing for qualitative inquiry: A relational approach*. New York, NY: Guilford Press.

Karnieli-Miller, O., Strier, R., & Pessach, L. (2009). Power relations in qualitative research. *Qualitative Health Research, 19*, 279–289. doi:10.1177/1049732308329306.

Kvale, S. (1996). *InterViews: An introduction to qualitative research inter-viewing*. Thousand Oaks, CA: Sage Publications.

Kvale, S. (2003, August). *Dialogical interview research – Emancipatory or oppressive?* Keynote speech at the 22nd meeting of the International Human Science Research Conference. Stockholm, Sweden.

Kvale, S. (2006). Dominance through interviews and dialogues. *Qualitative Inquiry, 12*(3), 480–500.

Mead, G.H. (1934). *Mind, self and society* (Vol. 111). Chicago, IL: University of Chicago Press.

Patton, M.Q. (2002). *Qualitative research and evaluation methods*. Thousand Oaks, CA: Sage Publications.

Scheurich, J.J. (1995). A postmodernist critique of research interviewing. *International Journal of Qualitative Studies in Education, 8*, 239–252. doi:10.1080/0951839950080303.

Tannen, D. (1993). *Framing in discourse*. New York, NY: Oxford University Press on Demand.

Vitus, K. (2008). The agonistic approach: Reframing resistance in qualitative research. *Qualitative Inquiry, 14*(3), 466–488.

Watzlawick, P., Bavelas, J.B., & Jackson, D.D. (1983, 2011). *Pragmatics of human communication: A study of interactional patterns, pathologies and paradoxes*. New York, NY: WW Norton & Company.

Watzlawick, P., Weakland, J.H., & Fisch, R. (1974). *Change: Principles of problem formation and problem resolution*. New York, NY: WW Norton & Company.

9 Reciprocity: The Nature and Attributes of Research Relations and Power

In this chapter, we suggest using the concept of reciprocity as research relations' defining attribute, regardless of their symmetry or asymmetry, and as a source of knowledge construction in qualitative research. Before we get to the construct of reciprocity, let us quickly review the relevant ideas that we developed in previous chapters. Whereas in the past, research participants were mainly considered to be providers of information (informants, subjects) and as means to an end of knowledge acquisition initiated by the researcher, fundamentally shaping asymmetrical relations, more recent conceptions of research relations attempt to create more symmetrical relations between researchers and participants. As a reaction to the initial asymmetric and potentially exploitative nature of research relations, a new trend has been developed, over the years, in which a quest for symmetry of relationships became a driving force and a sometimes goal of research (Kvale, 2003; Limerick, Burgess-Limerick, & Grace, 1996).

We claim that equality between research parties is unrealistic because each plays an entirely different role and is motivated by different drives. Adopting conceptions of the research relationship as symmetric or asymmetric tends to create interminable, futile attempts to achieve symmetry where it does not and cannot exist. Rather than viewing an egalitarian research system of relationships as reflecting a first-order change within the relationship, we suggest a second-order change in our construction of the research relationship system. Rather than restricting ourselves to either symmetrical or asymmetrical relationships, understanding these relations as reciprocal fosters a synthesis between the two previously opposing views. Using a dialectical reasoning mode, we switch from an either/or perspective to a both/and perspective (Basseches, 2005).

As discussed in Chapter 8, the conduct of research used to assume asymmetry between the research parties. As Reason (1994) so eloquently put it, "In traditional research, the roles of researcher and subject are mutually exclusive: the researcher alone contributes the thinking that goes into the project, and the subjects contribute the action or contents to be studied" (p. 42). Participants are mainly considered to be providers of information, a means to an end of knowledge acquisition initiated by the researcher. Indeed, popular wisdom maintains that as the persons asking the questions, researchers might be viewed as being in a more powerful position. Later, mainly for ethical considerations, the quest for symmetry was a reaction to the initial asymmetric and exploitative nature of research relationships. The initiative came from concerned scholars who sought to ameliorate historical wrongs (e.g., Edwards & Mautner, 2004; Manderson, Bennett, & Andajani-Sutjahjo, 2006; Oakley, 1981) that made power distribution in research dichotomous and asymmetrical in favor of the researcher, creating the possibility of exploitation (Karnieli-Miller, Strier, & Pessach, 2009; Limerick et al., 1996).

Many scholars took a critical position, emphasizing power gaps, trying to bridge those through egalitarianism and empowerment of participants. Taking the critical position, feminist researchers and those advocating participatory action research (PAR) have attempted to empower specific disadvantaged populations by advocating research relations based on an egalitarian partnership (e.g., Brayton, 1997; Maguire, 1987; Treleaven, 1994). Such perceptions of research relationships can be understood as having been derived from differences or similarities between researcher and participant (e.g., Aléx & Hammarström, 2007; Karnieli-Miller et al., 2009; Vitos, 2008). These could be either static (Ribens, 1989; Vitos, 2008) or dynamic (Aléx & Hammarström, 2007). In the static view of power differentials the researcher is traditionally presented as holding power over the participant (Kvale, 2003). In contrast, the dynamic view of power relations between researchers and participants indicates that first-order changes might occur throughout or even within different stages of the research process. Such a view might either refer to changes throughout the research process or to micro-changes occurring at a given stage. While not disproving such approaches, we have also suggested evaluating and making use of gaps between researcher and participants as a source of knowledge construction (See Chapters 6 and 7; Ben-Ari & Enosh, 2011; Enosh & Ben-Ari, 2010).

Ontologically, one cannot ignore the inherent power differentials in most research relationships. Epistemologically, the nature of research relations might be used as a source of the knowledge produced and affects the process of knowledge construction. At the same time, the ethical stances and epistemological considerations of the scholars involved influence the range of meanings attached to such differentials, and the ways proposed to cope with them are also influenced by the ethical stances and epistemological considerations of these same scholars. From an ethical standpoint, advocates of egalitarianism as an ultimate goal aspire to alleviate the problem by reducing the power gaps between the researcher and participants (e.g., Karnieli-Miller et al., 2009; Kvale, 1996, 2003; Oakley, 1981; Strier, 2006). Other scholars, for pragmatic reasons of knowledge acquisition, have tried to overcome participants' resistance by minimizing social gaps between them and the researcher (Cannell & Kahn, 1968; Oakley, 1981). In a classic paper, anticipating those developments in research relations' advocacy, Cannel and Kahn (1968) argued that "it may be best to minimize the social distance between interviewer and interviewee so that the interviewer is seen as within the range of communication of the respondent" (p. 585).

A question to be asked in this context is: "Are those power differences harmful to the participants and to knowledge production?" That there are power differentials between researcher and participants is an ontological fact. Seeing it as a disadvantage or an advantage is an ethical matter. So far, we have focused on views critical of the disadvantages and drawbacks that derive from it and thus have recommended reducing the gap on the ontological level. The critical approach assumes inherently or explicitly that equality (egalitarianism) is an ethical meta-goal to be pursued in all contexts.

With that, taking a different ethical and epistemological approach, we have emphasized the possible advantages of the gap. From our perspective, a social gap, and the power shifts between researchers and participants, can enrich the research project as far as knowledge construction is concerned. When researchers and participants were too similar, or too much in agreement, they would tend to trivialize the phenomena studied and the need to explore them. Their sense of differentness is dulled. Over-empathizing, and too much social and/or experiential closeness to the participants, reduces the researcher's genuine curiosity as well as the ability to reflect on the information and the life situation of the participants, thereby taking for granted what otherwise could have produced new insights. Status differentials and power shifts facilitate the search and inquisitiveness of the research partners, leading to the construction of knowledge. Within this framework, we echo Riben's (1989) question:

> How desirable is it, then, that we are socially close to the people we are interviewing? . . . What we need, perhaps, is sensitivity

to the ways in which particular social characteristics will affect our research relationships. How this affects the balance of power in the interview may be very significant for the talk that ensues. (1989, p. 581)

The idea of power differentials and power relations, and attempts to change this balance of power by trying to create an egalitarian research system, can be viewed as attempts at first-order change. Focusing on the interactions between researchers and participants would allow for schemata changes. The transition from viewing research relations in terms of the parties' roles to understanding the nature of research relationships gives rise to a second-order change in understanding them. Rather than restricting ourselves to either symmetrical or asymmetrical relationships, understanding these relations as *reciprocal* fosters a synthesis between the two previously opposing views. Using a dialectical reasoning mode, we switch from an either/or perspective to a both/and – a beyond dichotomy – perspective (Basseches, 2005).

The Reciprocity Norm: A Defining Attribute of the Research Relationship

Before showing how reciprocity relates to our view of the research relationship, a short theoretical presentation of the construct is in order. Reciprocity (2009) can be understood as a relationship of mutual dependence, action, or influence – a mutual or cooperative interchange of favors or privileges, especially the exchange of rights or privileges. In his classic paper, Gouldner (1960) distinguished between three meanings of reciprocity: first, as a pattern of mutually contingent exchanges of gratification; second, the existential or folk belief in reciprocity; and, third, the generalized moral norm. Based on this conceptualization, Uehara (1995) suggested two basic connotations for the reciprocity concept: a pattern of *social exchange of goods and services* and the moral belief in the *generalized obligatory norm*.

Within this context, three alternative explanations were suggested, implying three different moral meanings of reciprocity. The first is the *egoistic approach*, encouraging reciprocity as a way to increase one's benefits over time (Blau, 1964; Etzioni, 1988). Adhering to the *egoistic approach* implies that it is reasonable to realize the opportunity to over-benefit from an exchange. *Equity* is the pivotal attribute in the second approach (McClintock, Kramer, & Keil, 1984; Prinse, Buunk, & van Yperen, 1993; Walster, Walster, & Berschied, 1978), positing equality of the exchange as the rule. That is, when individuals adhering to the *equity* meaning of reciprocity are forced to choose between over-benefiting and under-benefiting from an exchange, they would prefer to over-benefit. The third is the *reciprocal approach* (Morris & Rosen, 1973; O'Connell, 1984; Uehara, 1990, 1995), drawing on the *norm of reciprocity*, implying that reciprocity, the ability to repay in kind, is of utmost importance, and, if forced to choose, individuals would prefer to under-benefit rather than to feel indebted.

Contextualizing the construct of reciprocity within our discussion, we assert that the norm of reciprocity stems from the common interest of both research parties to understand in-depth the phenomenon in question. Thus, reciprocity is a process whereby each research party believes that he or she contributes – not necessarily to the other party – but to a matter of common interest, an issue of concern, a social phenomenon, or a personal matter. From the researchers' perspectives, this is manifested in their interest in understanding the participants, learning about their worldviews and developing and constructing new knowledge.

When we consider participants' perspectives, the interest might be in egoistic as well as reciprocal benefits: sharing experiences with an empathic listener (Buckle, Dwyer, & Jackson, 2010; Campbell, Adams, Wasco, Ahrens, & Sefl, 2010; McCoyd & Shdaimah, 2007); feeling justified and vindicated through knowing that others share the same condition (Harper & Cole, 2012); voicing one's marginalized and stigmatized condition and discourse (McCoyd & Shdaimah, 2007); the opportunity to reflect on and derive meaning from one's experience (Dyregrov et al., 2011); or helping others in the same situation or condition are just a few of the reasons participants reported as motives for participating in qualitative research. Mutual interest, then, is the basis for understanding the inherent reciprocal nature of the exchange in research relations.

Therefore, rather than focusing on the relationships between researcher and participants, we focus on the relations between each party and the subject under study. This understanding creates a situation of similarity between the partners despite actual power differentials. From a different perspective, it is a second-order change because it not only involves relationships between human beings, but relationships between them and the subject of common interest as well.

The extensive literature on reciprocity in experimental and qualitative research demonstrates that, overall, most participants in reciprocity studies preferred reciprocal interactions or avoided interactions in which they over-benefited. Furthermore, in contrast to Gouldner's

(1960) assumption emphasizing immediate exchange, Ekeh (1974) argued that reciprocity need not be realized here and now. There might be time lags between giving and receiving, and they might include the possibility of indirect reciprocity (Uehara, 1995), as many ethnographic studies have demonstrated (Schreiber & Glideweel, 1978; Wentowski, 1981). Applying the reciprocity concept to contexts of power differences between actors in the exchange, Gouldner stated:

> Egotistic motivations may seek to get benefits without returning them . . . the situation is then ripe for the breakdown of reciprocity and for the development of . . . exploitation. The norm . . . safeguards powerful people against temptations of their own status; it motivates and regulates reciprocity as an exchange pattern, serving to inhibit the emergence of exploitative relations. (1960, p. 174)

This claim could be overly optimistic, given the abundance of exploitative situations in our world. However, we can certainly claim that the reciprocity norm has lessened the abuse of power in research relations, even if did not totally prevent it. Indeed, regarding our issues, the history of research ethics is rich in examples of power exploited by researchers (e.g., Guillemin & Gillam, 2004; Seto, 2001) – persons not motivated by this norm but probably by the egoistic moral code. However, the development of growing concern for research ethics and, as we discussed above, the movement that stresses egalitarianism in research relations (e.g., Baum, MacDougall, & Smith, 2006; Karnieli-Miler et al., 2009; Kvale, 2003) emphasizes the equity principle, attempting to achieve egalitarianism and a direct reciprocal exchange between researchers and those they research. As Uehara pointed out, recipients who had not had an opportunity to reciprocate either directly or indirectly reported "feelings of discomfort, guilt, inadequacy and even resentment" (Uehara, 1995, p. 490).

It is possible that scholars and researchers who emphasize equity are driven by feelings of guilt and discomfort in over-benefiting from the exchange and by collective guilt over abuses of power by other researchers. Since such attempts to achieve a form of direct reciprocity and egalitarianism have largely been futile, we suggest perceiving relations between the researcher and participants as based on indirect reciprocity, in which each party brings different forms of expert knowledge to the exchange. Reciprocity allows for asymmetrical relations, be they static or dynamic, while enabling each research party to gain from them. Power differentials are acknowledged and exchanges between the parties are promoted. Each recognizes his or her contribution to the research process, as well as that of the other party.

Producing knowledge can be perceived as a joint venture of the researcher and the participant, so that reciprocity can be thought of as a defining attribute of the research relationship. The researchers benefit directly from the exchange, whereas the participants probably benefit directly and/or indirectly in the long run, rather than directly and immediately. Thus, reciprocity might be affected indirectly by using the constructed knowledge later to help those participants or others in similar situations. Characterizing the research relationships as reciprocal, we inevitably consider the need for mutual recognition and respect, knowing that advancing the topic in question is contingent upon the contribution of each party. That is, understanding the reciprocal nature of research relations entails mutual respect.

References

Aléx, L., & Hammarström, A. (2007). Shifts in power during an interview situation: Methodological reflections inspired by Foucault and Bourdieu. *Journal of Nursing Inquiry, 15*, 169–176. doi:10.1111/j.1440–1800.2008.00398.x.

Basseches, M. (2005). The development of dialectical thinking as an approach to integration. *Integral Review, 1*, 47–63.

Baum, F., MacDougall, C., & Smith, D. (2006). Participatory action research. *Journal of Epidemiology and Community Health, 60*, 854–857. doi:10.1136/jech.2004.028662.

Ben-Ari, A., & Enosh, G. (2011). Processes of reflectivity: Knowledge construction in qualitative research. *Qualitative Social Work, 10*, 152–171. doi:10.1177/1473325010369024.

Blau, P. (1964). *Exchange and power in social life.* New York, NY: John Wiley & Sons.

Brayton, J. (1997). *What makes feminist research feminist? The structure of feminist research within the social sciences.*

Buckle, J.L., Dwyer, S.C., & Jackson, M. (2010). Qualitative bereavement research: Incongruity between the perspectives of participants and research ethics boards. *International Journal of Social Research Methodology, 13*, 111–125. doi:10.1080/13645570902767918.

Campbell, R., Adams, A.E., Wasco, S.M., Ahrens, C.E., & Sefl, T. (2010). What has it been like for you to talk with me today? The impact of participating in interview research on rape survivors. *Violence Against Women, 16*, 60–83. doi:10.1177/1077801209353576.

Cannell, C.E., & Kahn, R.L. (1968). Interviewing. In L. Gardner & E. Aronson (Eds.), *The handbook of social psychology* (Vol. 2, 2nd ed., pp. 526–595). Reading, MA: Addison Wesley.

Dyregrov, K.M., Dieserud, G., Hjelmeland, H.M., Straiton, M., Rasmussen, M.L., Knizek, B.L., & Leenaars, A.A. (2011). Meaning-making through psychological autopsy interviews: The value of participating in qualitative research for those bereaved by suicide. *Death Studies, 35*, 685–710.

Edwards, R., & Mautner, M. (2004). Ethics and feminist research: Theory and practice. In M.L. Mauthner, M. Birch, J. Jessop, & T. Miller (Eds.), *Ethics in qualitative research* (pp. 14–31). London: Sage Publications.

Ekeh, P.P. (1974). *Social exchange theory: The two traditions.* Cambridge, MA: Harvard University Press.

Enosh, G., & Ben-Ari, A. (2010). Cooperation and conflict in qualitative research: A dialectical approach to knowledge production. *Qualitative Health Research, 20*, 125–130. doi:10.1177/1049732309348503.

Etzioni, A. (1988). *The moral dimension: Towards a new economics.* New York, NY: Free Press.

Gouldner, A. (1960). The norm of reciprocity: A preliminary statement. *American Sociological Review, 25*, 161–178. doi:10.2307/2092623.

Guillemin, M., & Gillam, L. (2004). Ethics, reflexivity, and 'ethically important moments' in research. *Qualitative Inquiry, 10*, 261–280. doi:10.1177/1077800403262360.

Harper, M., & Cole, P. (2012). Member checking: Can benefits be gained similar to group therapy? *Qualitative Report, 17*, 510–517. Retrieved from www.nova.edu/ssss/QR/ QR17–2/harper.pdf.

Karnieli-Miller, O., Strier, R., & Pessach, L. (2009). Power relations in qualitative research. *Qualitative Health Research, 19*, 279–289. doi:10.1177/1049732308329306.

Kvale, S. (1996). *InterViews: An introduction to qualitative research interviewing.* Thousand Oaks, CA: Sage Publications.

Kvale, S. (2003, August). *Dialogical interview research – Emancipatory or oppressive*? Keynote speech at the 22nd meeting of the International Human Science Research Conference. Stockholm, Sweden.

Limerick, B., Burgess-Limerick, T., & Grace, M. (1996). The politics of interviewing: Power relations and accepting the gift. *Qualitative Studies in Education, 9*, 449–460. doi:10.1080/0951839960090406.

Maguire, P. (1987). *Doing participatory research: A feminist approach.* Amherst, MA: University of Massachusetts Press.

Manderson, L., Bennett, E., & Andajani-Sutjahjo, S. (2006). The social dynamics of the interview: Age, class, and gender. *Qualitative Health Research, 16*, 1317–1334. doi:10.1177/1049732306294512.

McClintock, C.G., Kramer, R.M., & Keil, L.J. (1984). Equity and social exchange in human relationships. *Advances in Experimental Social Psychology, 17*, 183–228. doi:10.1016/ S0065–2601.

McCoyd, J.L.M., & Shdaimah, C.S. (2007). Revisiting the benefits debate: Salubrious effects of social work research. *Social Work, 52*, 340–349.

84   *Relational Implications – Power Relationships*

Morris, S. C., & Rosen, S. (1973). Effects of felt adequacy and opportunity to reciprocate on help seeking. *Journal of Experimental and Social Psychology*, *9*, 265–276. doi:10.1016/0022–1031(73)90015–2.

Oakley, A. (1981). Interviewing women: A contradiction in terms. In H. Roberts (Ed.), *Doing feminist research* (pp. 30–61). London: Routledge & Kegan Paul.

O'Connell, L. (1984). An exploration of exchange in three social relationships: Kinship, friendships and the marketplace. *Journal of Social and Personal Relationships*, *1*, 333–345. doi:10.1177/0265407584013006.

Prinse, K.S., Buunk, B.P., & van Yperen, N.W. (1993). Equity normative disapproval and extramarital relationships. *Journal of Social and Personal Relationships*, *10*, 39–53. doi:10.1177/0265407593101003.

Reason, P. (1994). *Participation in human inquiry*. London: Sage Publications.

Ribens, J. (1989). Interviewing – An 'unnatural situation'? *Women's Studies International Forum*, *12*, 579–592. doi:10.1016/0277–5395(89)90002–2.

Schreiber, S., & Glideweel, J.C. (1978). Social norms and helping in a community of limited liability. *American Journal of Community Psychology*, *6*, 441–453. doi: 10.1007/bf00941420.

Seto, B. (2001). History of medical ethics and perspectives on disparities in minority recruitment and involvement in health research. *American Journal of the Medical Science*, *322*, 246–250.

Strier, R. (2006). Anti-oppressive research in social work: A preliminary definition. *British Journal of Social Work*, *37*, 857–871. doi:10.1093/bjsw/bcl062.

Treleaven, L. (1994). Making a space: A collaborative inquiry with women as staff development. In P. Reason (Ed.), *Participation in human inquiry* (pp. 138–162). London: Sage Publications.

Uehara, E.S. (1990). Dual exchange theory, social networks, and informal social support. *American Journal of Sociology*, *96*, 521–527. doi:10.1086/229571.

Uehara, E.S. (1995). Reciprocity reconsidered: Gouldner's 'Moral Norm of Reciprocity' and social support. *Journal of Social and Personal Relationships*, *12*, 483–502. doi:10.1177/0265407595124001.

Vitos, K. (2008). The agonistic approach: Reframing resistance in qualitative research. *Qualitative Inquiry*, *14*, 466–488. doi:10.1177/1077800407309331.

Walster, E., Walster, G.W., & Berschied, E. (1978). *Equity: Theory and research*. Boston, MA: Ellyn & Bacon.

Wentowski, G. (1981). Reciprocity and the coping strategies of older people: Cultural dimensions of network building. *Gerontologist*, *21*, 600–608. doi:10.1093/geront/21.6.600.

10 Epilogue

From Dialectics to Dialog Across Liminal Spaces

There is an old Indian fable of blind monks encountering an elephant. The first feels the tusks and concludes that they have encountered an old and fearsome weapon. The second feels the leg and concludes they are in the ruins of an old temple. The third feels the tail and concludes it is a rope. The fourth feels the trunk and warns them all that they have encountered a boa constrictor and should run away.

The chapters of the book represent different aspects of a complete whole. Reading each of the chapters on its own may disrupt the underlying logic of the book. Although each can be considered separately or independently, they should be considered in their entirety. Otherwise, their comprehensive meaning, context, and applications may be lessened.

Every philosophical tradition is defined and distinguished by the answers it provides to three major questions: What is reality/existence (ontology/metaphysics)? How do we know it (epistemology)? And what should we do about it and how should we behave (ethics/morality)? Within this framework, the present book deals with these three questions and, as such, is situated within the philosophical arena. This is not accidental, as we both shared the assumption that research methods are a practical implementation of philosophical positions.

The book starts with a presentation of our basic constructivist worldview through raising the metaphor of maps and territories and remembering that a map is never the territory itself but a representation of the model one holds regarding reality (Korzybski, 1933). Human knowledge and understanding is always just a map of the reality to which it refers and every map symbolizes certain pragmatic aspects, while neglecting all other aspects. What is being represented and what is being neglected is the result of a prior schema held by an interested human agent. Thus, the different chapters of this book are like different maps of the complex reality of the qualitative research realm. Furthermore, it is important to emphasize that there are still many areas within this enchanted realm we call qualitative research that we have never reached and other areas that have yet to be mapped.

A major part of knowledge construction is the construct of dialectics. Dialectics is a key used for understanding and mapping social reality. As with every "lock and key," there may be various and different keys that open the same lock, some of which look and feel completely different from others. Still, all of those would open the lock. Our use of dialectical means is just one of those keys. In a nutshell, we define dialectics as a framework wherein contrasts and apparent contradictions at a certain level may be understood and unified at a higher level of conceptualizing and understanding. Furthermore, dialectics emphasizes change; it goes beyond static structures to direct our construction of the world as an ongoing process and movement. Human beings – researchers and participants – have a tendency to observe the world (or, to be more accurate, to construct the world) in static terms, to define structures. However, what may seem to be a stable, unchanging reality is but a construct and underlying it are constant change and movement. This is true for the physical world and, much more so, for the social one. This conceptualization refers mainly to the ontological aspect of our inquiry.

From dialectics, we moved on to dwell on processes of reflectivity (or reflexivity, as some might call it). While we perceive dialectics as a "master key" for analyzing personal, interpersonal, and social phenomena, focusing on dialectic processes alone may mistakenly be understood as taking a mechanistic view of human affairs. However, much of humans' interactions with each other, with the world, and with themselves is based on the ways by which they construct their understanding of what is going on; their ways of awareness, their processes of reflectivity. Reflectivity is the key construct for understanding used by both researchers and participants. We discussed the idea of "sense of differentness" – as a basic dialectical starting point for the reflective process, for the production of knowledge. The starting point from which, using dialectical means such as noticing apparent contradictions, incompleteness, figure and ground, and other means, reflectivity may progress from observation, through accounting, deliberation, and reconstruction to higher levels of conceptualization and the integration of knowledge.

In our book, we have highlighted the instrumental role reflectivity plays in the construction of new knowledge. Indeed, reflectivity is a significant part of the human conduct, which can be utilized by all parties involved in the research process, to reach higher and deeper levels of understanding. That is, researchers are not the only ones to take part in reflective processes. We believe that the unique contribution of research participants goes beyond the provision of information, but rather the provision of information is enhanced through their own processes of reflectivity. Emphasizing the active enhancement and the search for outcomes of both researchers' and participants' reflectivity is probably one of the unique contributions of our book. Participants' reflectivity is affected by their willingness to approach or distance themselves from lived experience and may move back and forth between different levels of proximity and distancing. Such conceptualization highlights the epistemological aspects of our book.

Departing from the "individual" level analysis of reflective processes, we continue our line of thinking by shifting focus to the interactive relationships between researchers and participants, therefore reaching the ethical aspects of our conceptualization. Research relations may be conceptualized and understood from various perspectives. Those perspectives include (but are not limited to) status and power differences, control of knowledge, and differences in moral stances, all of which are various maps of the ways by which interactions by research partners contribute to knowledge production. All of these have contributed to our view that research relations can be thought of as being reciprocal in nature. Viewing reciprocity as the defining attribute of the research relations bypasses the old debate regarding symmetric and/or asymmetric relations between researchers and participants. The consideration of relationships between researchers and participants reflects a moral perspective, thus bringing the ethical aspects of research into this work. Yet, whereas such considerations take an outsider (etic) view regarding the morality of relationships within research, as researchers and methodologists we need also to consider the moral inner (emic) moral perspectives of the researchers and participants themselves and how the interaction of those moral stances affects the processes of knowledge construction.

In this sense, the entire book is about research ethics and moral stances; as it is about reflexivity; as it is about dialectics. It is about research relationships being the key to conducting and understanding research. One metaphor that bridges all these issues is the metaphor of liminal space. When we talk about a dialectical tension between constructions of reality, we talk about the need to first comprehend and then to bridge the liminal space between seemingly contradictory concepts or realities. When we discuss reflectivity emerging from sense of differentness, we talk about being aware of the liminal space of an apparent incongruity. When we talk about research relations, we talk about the liminal space between researchers and participants (and other stakeholders in the research endeavor). Liminal space between human beings, be it researchers and participants, or any others, may be conceived in the terminology that Martin Buber coined as the "in between" (Buber, 1965). Discussing human relations, he suggested that two types of relations may exist – "I–it" relations and "I–thou" relations. The I–it relation is instrumental as it refers to such relations that exist between "subject" and "object," reflecting the agenda of one or the two sides. Indeed, most human relations, research relations included, are I–it relations; for, as Buber stated, without I–it relations, no human life could survive. However, he continues that without I–thou ("subject" to "subject" relations) relations, life would not be human and would lose its meaning and significance.

In this book, we have tried to point out many of the subtle ways that qualitative research is an I–it endeavor, highlighting the immense contributions of the I–it approach to the production of knowledge. However, we cannot conclude this book without emphasizing the role of I–thou approach in making research relations dialogical and therefore humane. Friedman (1985), who dedicated so much of his work to the understanding of Buber's philosophy, indicates that true I–thou moments are rare occurrences. Paradoxically, if the dialog is conducted with the constant expectation for an I–thou moment to occur, the entire dialog essentially becomes I–it relations, for which the I–thou is the expected outcome. Obviously, an I–thou moment would not, and could not, arise in such a context. However, an I–thou approach can be taken without expecting it to lead to such peak experiences and that would lead to a dialogical relation. By assuming such an approach, the researcher facilitates a true meeting with the participants and other stakeholders in the research endeavor, promoting the I–it goal of knowledge construction.

Before we conclude, we would like to address the practical implications of this book. Both of us are teachers of research methods (qualitative and quantitative) and both of us are supervisors of graduate students. There have been many times that both of us have faced the challenge of departing from the descriptive level to the theoretical one. In this book, we have tried to create text that eventually helps students of qualitative research methods to train themselves in going beyond the apparent and self-evident and beyond the semi-dichotomies that pervade the everyday research thinking. We hope that this has been helpful.

References

Buber, M. (1965). *The knowledge of men.* New York, NY: Macmillan Company.

Friedman, M. S. (1985). *The healing dialog in psychotherapy.* New York, NY: Jason Aronson.

Korzybski, A. (1933). *Science and sanity: An introduction to non-Aristotelian systems and general semantics.* Englewood, NJ: Institute of General Semantics.

Index

research partners, researchers as 33, 37–39
research phases 68–69
research relationships: asymmetrical 76–77; egalitarian 6, 76–77, 81; frames of reference 5, 65–74; I-it versus I-thou relations 88; interactional nature of 65–67; interaction styles 5, 69–74; misleading or false dichotomies of 66; nature of 4; passive 65–66; power differentials 4–5, 57–63, 67–68, 77–79; practical implications 88; reciprocity 5–6, 76–82; role in knowledge construction 87; symmetrical 6, 61, 76–77; triadic system of 2
Ribens, J. 78
Ridgeway, C.L. 58

second-order change: concept of 18–19; reflectivity as 29–30; in research relationships 6, 73, 76, 79–80
self-evident subject matter, agreement on 48–49
"sense of differentness" 3–4, 24–25, 86–87
shifting focus of participants 44–46
social constructivism 13

social exchange of goods and services, reciprocity in 79
social status: concept of 59–60; power differentials and 61–63
stakeholder relationships *see* research relationships
state of mind 24
status: concept of 58–59; hierarchies 60; power differentials and 61–63
symmetrical research relationships 6, 61, 76–77
synthesis, fostering 6, 18–19, 27, 30, 66, 76, 79
systemic aspects of communication 35–36, 52–53

"taken-for-granted" attitude 48–49
trivialization 44–45
turning points 28

Uehara, E.S. 79
utilitarian action plans 13

Vitus, K. 36, 51, 70
von Glaserfeld, Ernst 13, 16, 23, 28

Walker, H.A. 58
Watzlawick, P. 18, 29, 35, 52
Weakland, J.H. 18, 29
Weber, M. 58